The Piñata Theory™

by Charlene Renaud

The Piñata Theory™ What's In Your Stuffing?
Unleash the Power of Your Subconscious Mind, Smash Adversity and Rock Your Piñata!

Canadian Intellectual Property Office | An Agency of Industry Canada

The Piñata Theory™
Trademark Filing No.: 1870694™ 2017
Copyright Registration No.: 1138723 © 2017

Disclaimer
This book contains the ideas and opinions of its author. The intention of this book is to provide information, helpful content and motivation to readers about on the subjects addressed. It is shared and sold with the understanding that the author is not engaged to render any type of psychological, medical, legal or any other kind of personal or professional advice. No warranties or guarantees are expressed or implied by the author's choice to include any of the content in this volume. The reader should always consult his or her medical, health or other professional and accredited health provider before adopting any of the suggestions in this book or drawing any ideas, inferences or practices from this book. The author shall not be liable for any physical, psychological, emotional, financial or commercial damages, including, but not limited to, special, incidental, consequential or other damages. The reader is responsible for their own choices, actions and results.

1st Edition, 1st printing 2018

Cover design by Christine Strydom
Interior design by Steve Walters at Carolyn Flower International - www.carolynflower.com
Cover illustration by Christine Strydom
Interior illustrations by Vazha Kurkhuli
Author photo by Heike Delmore - Delmore Creative / Couture Portrait

ISBN-13: 978-1986075466 (CreateSpace-Assigned)
ISBN-10: 198607546X

Dedicated to the Loves of My Life:
My Children, Lisa and Jordan

I Am Blessed by You, I Am Proud of You

Be Guided by Your Inner Light –
Embrace the Seed of Greatness Within

Be Grateful All Days

Charlene Renaud - The Piñata Theory™

What's in Charlene's Stuffing?

In the following pages, I share slices of my life journey – the highs, life shattering blows, and the discovery that my broken Piñata needed a major stuffing-overhaul.

For years, I barely scratched the surface of confronting the root of my pain. I knew, whatever the source, it was deep, profound, and at times paralyzing. My spring of dysfunction and automatic behavior, bubbled from an ocean of multi-faceted life experiences, stored deep within the subconscious mind.

To solve the riddle, I invested in a psychologist – Manny from Montreal. Within five minutes of our first meeting, Manny had me pegged. Months into self-discovery, I was successful in identifying and evolving beyond the unresolved issues that were hidden beneath the surface of my conscious life.

Sharing this discovery with my friend, I said, *I burst open my subconscious mind, like bursting open a Piñata.* This was my *Piñata-Ah-Ha Moment.* I wanted to share this breakthrough with others, to help them heal and evolve into their healthiest state of being.

With the aid of a Piñata, I share the incredible depth, flexibility and powerful grip of the subconscious mind — a storage bin containing every grain of life experience.

Your mind can be your best friend or your biggest setback. To this end, I ask, *What's in Your Stuffing?* I cover multiple sources of stuffing and how it affects an individual, families, communities and the world.

The Piñata Theory™ challenges you to step out of normalcy, into thirsting for personal and global transformation.

A powerful message for humanity is laid out, like a puzzle, piece by piece, starting with an incredible vision in my childhood. As the story progresses, the prophetic significance of this event becomes clear — unfolding beautifully through a timely sequence of events.

Throughout my life, I have experienced divine intervention and experiences that defy rational explanation. Gratefully, these incredible moments provided me with unshakable clarity — God is the source of life, love and truth. We are more than flesh.

My life purpose was spoken into the universe decades ago. My cousin Rachelle, and I, laid on a hill, one sunny summer day at my farmstead near Comber, Ontario, Canada. We dreamingly gazed at the fluffy white clouds, set against the blue canvas sky, sharing childhood dreams of our picture-perfect future life. I recall, vividly seeing myself on stage — singing, and speaking, standing in front of *thousands* of people. I voiced what I had seen, heard, and felt, in this moment, to Rachelle. I confidently hurled my wish-boomerang into the sky.

The universe heard and responded, providing the pathway to my destiny. Yet, life-altering and traumatic events threw my Piñata into a tailspin. Crushed mentally, spiritually, physically and emotionally, I held on to the strength of God's love. Step by step, day by day, I began a challenging, yet rehabilitating process. This experience became my launchpad into a new paradigm, and eventually gave birth to *The Piñata Theory™*.

My mission is to empower multitudes of Piñatas…no matter where you've been, what you've done, or what others have done to you — it's time to return to your inherent greatness. Tear jerking, mind-altering revelations found in *The Piñata Theory™*, reveal the pathway to freedom, peace, love, healing and forgiveness.

Throughout the book, a love story unravels, supporting *The Piñata Theory's™* main message: You can remain as you are — dominated by your past, or you can consciously choose to change, operating and flourishing from the seed of greatness planted within.

Liberation is possible. It begins by connecting to a higher power, being spiritually lead, directing your mind, and rearranging your stuffing!

The Piñata Theory™
Piñata-Lingo

Charlene's Unique Piñata Language used in The Piñata Theory™

Piñata Purpose – Your life purpose, your gifts that make you unique and special. You share these gifts and your stuffing with other Piñatas to make the world a better place.

Distraction Piñata – Piñatas who annoy you, bother you, tempt you, distract you, or piss you off. They come into your life to derail you. Avoid time with these Piñatas. When you come across one, scream in your head, *DISTRACTION!* This moves the conscious mind into action. You won't allow this Piñata to bother you, annoy you, tempt you, distract you or piss you off, because you got their number.

Energy Sucking Piñata – A Piñata who sucks the stuffing out of you, leaving you breathless, exhausted and perplexed. An example of this breed of Piñata: *The Drama Piñata*. They suck you into their drama and before you know it, you get tangled in their stuff. Avoid this Piñata as well.

Bye-Bye Piñata – A Piñata you want and need to say bye-bye to, such as a *Distraction Piñata* and an *Energy Sucking Piñata*.

Sheep Piñata – A Piñata who follows other Piñatas without consciously questioning the status quo. They tend to follow the crowd, and are mesmerized by shiny objects. They want to fit in and be accepted, to the point of losing their stuffing. They eat, drink and sleep and roll the same dice day in and day out. They are general consumers who have no inkling to work on community or global issues. Baaa.

Piñata Sheep Herder – These Piñatas are leaders. They know their purpose and live it fully. They exist to lead, inspire, mentor, teach, and help other Piñatas. Their spirit speaks boldly, sharing love, compassion and wisdom wherever they lead. They follow and serve one leader — God.

Flaming-Torch Piñata Tip – A *Sparkling Pinata Tip* is a flaming torch, meant to catch your attention, and fire up your stuffing. Example: Take inventory of your stuffing and where it came from, especially distorted views about different cultures. Discuss examples of historical and current racism with Piñatas (especially children), and how this affects countless others. It's like bullying, but on a wider and more vicious level, based on judging, mistreating, targeting and/or hurting people of another culture.

Jelly Bean Piñata Tip – A delicious life tip. Example: When we learn something new and better, yet we slide into old ways based on old stuffing, then we have one foot in our fluff. The subconscious mind is at play. Conscious over-ride is a deliberate action — choosing the new way, knowing that it has a reward or benefit over the old way.

Super-High-Powered-Piñata-Poop-Popper – Your super, high-powered weapon, used to destroy *Piñata Poop*.

Piñata Poop – All of the shitty stuffing you gathered throughout your lifetime.

More-Stuff-Piñata (MSP) – *The More-Stuff-Piñata* believes that happiness comes from collecting stuff. But, what the MSP hasn't thought through, is that all this stuff costs more money to have, to maintain, to insure, to clean, to fix. And, they have to work many hours to pay for this stuff, taking precious time away from family or healthier endeavors.

The MSP also feels important showing their stuff to other Piñatas. They wish to impress Piñatas with their possessions. This spirit-poor Piñata lives to make more money to buy more stuff, yet is truly not happy in the end. Money doesn't buy love or respect.

Baby Piñata – A baby Piñata up to the age of four.

Children Piñatas – The child of a *Parent Piñata*. Children are little people who hold the key to our future. Love, honor, teach, guide, and involve yourself in a healthy way, into their lives. They are precious beyond comprehension. Also referred to as *Piñata Cubs*. In the context of *The Piñata Theory™*, I refer to children who are pre-adult and under the direct care of a parent.

Parent Piñata – A human who has birthed, fathered, mothered or parented a child.

Piñata Survival Instinct – Your built-in automatic defense system that helps your Piñata survive under extreme duress or life-threatening situation. It is controlled by your subconscious mind and is meant to protect you. Not everyone has experienced this inner mechanism of survival. When you do, you will know.

Sub-Piñata State – Turning off the conscious mind and delving into the subconscious mind, through meditation, sleep or hypnosis.

Broken-Chooser Piñata – Your chooser is broken, meaning, you need to fix your chooser. You are picking people, things or substances based on unhealthy stuffing. Fixing your chooser entails dealing with your toxic stuffing, and downloading new healthy stuffing. When your chooser is healthy, you will choose a healthy mate, friend or tribe.

Piñata Ah Ha Moment – When you experience a life-changing, yellow-highlighter moment. This comes as a flash of realization, inspiration, insight, discovery or understanding. Your Piñata knows something just happened that stopped you in your hooves. You paid attention. You woke up. Something clicked in your stuffing. An example of a *Piñata Ah Ha Moment:* A Piñata experiences a deep appreciation for life, their body, and spirit while in recovery and would never go back to unbalanced ways. *The Piñata Ah Ha Moment* is appreciation for life, being fully present, and experiencing all of its beauty without distortion.

Superhero Piñata – A Piñata who feels compelled to continually rescue others, like a Superhero. We love heros, but this Piñata forgets to save and protect themself first.

Piñata-Cat – *A Piñata-Cat* gets only so many chances to land on their feet. Ultimately, their luck runs out. Poor kitty needs to pay attention and be careful.

Generational Stuffing – Stuffing that is relevant to the era you were born in. Belief and knowledge systems during your time on earth. Stuffing that can be passed from one generation to the next. Generational stuffing changes, as Piñatas acquire new knowledge. What is factual to one generation, may be outdated to another generation. Yet, this stuffing is what the Piñata downloaded, mostly consistent with Piñatas born in the same era. Imagine your Grandmothers era and yours, comparing the similarities and differences, as well as the news of the day. You will quickly conclude that generational stuffing is powerful. Examples of major generation groups: Greatest Generation, Baby Boomers, Generation X, Generation Y, Millennials.

Human-Made Stuffing or Human Stuffing – Stuffing from other humans, based on their generation, culture, education, geographical location, religion, racial beliefs, family dynamics, phobias and much more. Anything that came from the mind, hand or mouth of a human (alive or dead) that you heard, read, or witnessed.

God-Loaded-Stuffing or God's Amazing Stuffing – All that comes from God to you. He is the source of creation, endless love, truth and universal knowledge. His stuffing is flawless and unlimited, unlike *Human-Made Stuffing*.

Piñata-Shell – Your Piñata's body…made of bones, skin, muscles, cells, hair, a liver, a heart, lungs, teeth and a brain. All physical stuff that is touchable. Well, almost.

The Subconscious and Conscious Mind – The subconscious mind is a storage bin of everything you have experienced or learned in your lifetime. It operates your life systems automatically and is so vast, it cannot be measured. It is the underlying mind or sub-mind, as it runs in the background and can affect your everyday life, as it is so powerful. It has valuable stuffing or flawed stuffing. It stores information you can draw from at a later date. Data within this sub-mind is unfiltered, and was stored here, often without choice. The subconscious mind has no filter…everything goes in: the good, the bad and the ugly. It operates 24/7, even while you sleep. No one knows the extent of information within this mind. It is believed by some, to contain intelligence and experiences from your ancestry, embedded within your DNA.

Your conscious mind represents your thoughts in the moment, or in the now, that you use to make choices. Example: *Do I want a pizza or a salad?* This mind can over-ride the subconscious mind, meaning you can make choices based on newly discovered sources, versus drawing upon or trusting dated stuffing in your subconscious data bank. Conscious means awake. Wake up!

The Spirit holds the trump card over the subconscious and conscious mind. *Spirit Stuffing* is your inner voice, a piece of God planted within you. Spirit is your link to God. The Spirit speaks to you, through gentle whispers, a sudden thought or vision, or a knowing that protects and guides you. Wise Piñatas listen to their Spirit for direction.

The Spirit Stuffing is honest, pure truth. It is our inner *God-Positioning-System* (GPS) with unlimited data. Spirit is our means of connection to God.

The Grand Piñata – God of course.

Spirit-Walkers – Piñatas who are guided by spirit and flow through life in a purposeful, God serving way.

Piñata Radio – Think of your Piñata, as if it is a radio. Your Piñata tunes into channels that contain *Human-Made Stuffing* — human-based information absorbed by you, since birth. Your Piñata has a limited number of channels from human sources.

Super Spirit Antenna – Imagine you are a *Piñata Radio* equipped with a *Super Spirit Antenna*. This *Super Spirit Antenna* has a direct link to God. This is what Spirit is, your built-in *Super Spirit Antenna*, connected directly to God. With this *Super Spirit Antenna*, not only can you listen to God, you also have countless channels accessing universal knowledge and a built-in microphone to speak to God. And…God hears everything on your *Piñata Radio*. He listens to every word from your mouth, all thoughts in your mind, and each feeling deep in your heart.

God-Cast Channels – Wisdom from God that comes to you via the *Super Spirit Antenna* (your Spirit) directly to your *Piñata Radio*.

God's Soul Station – The source of unlimited knowledge and life guidelines for your Piñata. It's free, loving, forgiving, and life-changing. The hub of all greatness, where the impossible does not exist.

Piñata Decoder – Unravelling and compassionately examining the stuffing buried in your subconscious mind. The ability to be consciously aware of the impact of, and, what's been stuffed (or stored) inside of you. In doing so, you will understand how your stuffing impacts daily responses, behavior, health and potential. You will discover hidden treasures in your Piñata that positively influence you, as well as toxic stuffing that is harmful or unhealthy. Armed with this *Piñata Decoder*, you will be able to separate truth from myth and dramatically change your life for the better. Your Piñata will crave new healthy stuffing and learn to be conscious (aware) of your ability to create a beautiful life.

The Piñata Code™ — The realization that you are more than flesh, more than your mind and you are not confined within a limited human belief system. You are more than the sum total of what you have been told, experienced or seen from earthly sources. You are a spirit traveling in human form.

Precious Piñata – You are precious, and more valuable than pure gold or diamonds. You are loved, unique and totally awesome. You are the precious child of *The Greatest Piñata* — God. Walk in your inherent greatness — through spirit, in truth and love.

Free-Range Piñatas – *Free-Range Piñatas* choose to go their own way, and in the end, the summary of their choices becomes the story of their life. They frequently devour and make decisions based on human stuffing. Instant gratification is often a main influence without consideration of consequence to themselves or others. They are guided by flesh, rather than the spirit.

Boozy-the-Clown Piñata – A Piñata who is a party animal, whose main sport is drinking alcohol. He's (she's) a teenager – two, three, four times over and will likely never grow up.

Monkey Piñata See, Monkey Piñata Do – A Piñata who watches another Piñata and repeats patterns and behaviors of this Piñata. Similar to a *Sheep Piñata*, who mimics another.

A Piñata Conscious Over-Ride – Consciously applying newly learned knowledge, responses, and behavior, versus being trapped by repetitious patterns...doing the same thing over and over. The ability to over-ride and over-write the subconscious mind through conscious application of in-the-moment decision making. Using your authority to reject flawed, untruthful or harmful stuffing.

The Mammoth Piñata in the Room – Avoiding reality about a mammoth issue, by hiding the obvious. Refusing to address something you, the family or community knows is wrong. Not taking the steps to right a wrong that everyone is aware of. An obvious problem or difficult situation that Piñatas do not want to talk about. In the end, many Piñatas suffer.

Spiritual Piñatas – These are Piñatas who live through spirit. Their life purpose is to serve God. Their lives, actions and words are reflective of God's teaching.

Warrior Piñata – A *Warrior Piñata* is a brave Piñata, who has experienced struggle, yet showed perseverance and courage, fighting for a worthy cause. Piñatas who use their gifts, love and talent to teach, help and guide other Piñatas.

Bad-Ass Piñata – *The Rock* (Dwayne Johnson), is a fine example of this class of Piñata. Learn from Dwayne's words about struggle, "I like to use the hard times in the past to motivate me today." *Be a Bad-Ass Piñata* and remember to get up after hard times and show the world your beautiful colors.

Silly Piñata – A Piñata who repeats a behavior that he/she knows is wrong. You need to fire up *Piñata Conscious Over-Ride* to conquer your silliness.

Bullshit-Stuffing (BS-Stuffing) is avoiding facts and doing it anyway, or creating a false reality to cover the truth, to make situations look better than they actually are. BS-Stuffing is loaded with trouble.

Me-Agenda Stuffing is often the launch pad for *BS-Stuffing*. *Me-Agenda Stuffing* is self-satisfying, done without honest evaluation or concern for long-term consequences, or both. Eventually these scenarios backfire and cause pain to someone.

Gratefulness Stuffing – The more *Gratefulness Stuffing* we download and ultimately share, the happier and more satisfied we will be. To be grateful means to feel or show an appreciation of anything in your life; being thankful. *Gratefulness Stuffing* spreads kindness and appreciation to others.

Piñata La-La Land – Remaining in a state of denial or in a dreamy belief pattern that avoids reality. Applying dated and ineffective ways to address a problem.

Piñata Power – Let Your Best Stuffing Shine:

🍬 Not allowing others to define you or control your destiny.

🍬 Accepting that some situations are best left as is, because it's fruitless to continue. Consider who the players are. If they are set in their ways, are ego-driven or have personal agendas, you will lose, even if you score on them or win.

🍬 God has final judgement. Let go, let God.

- Walk away with your head held high versus challenging a machine you know will make your life difficult or create roadblocks.
- Trusting universal law — all is balanced, eventually. We reap what we give.
- Get your game on — shake the dust off your stuffing and get up!
- You have natural gifts and talents that make you feel awesome. Keep doing what brings you joy and blesses others.
- Pray. Forgive. Learn. Move Forward.

Piñata Role Model – A Piñata who focuses their actions and words on kindness and love. A Piñata looked to by others as an example to be imitated. They have success in any of these areas: wellness, love, sobriety, relationships, entrepreneurship, leadership, bravery, perseverance, and/or overcoming great odds.

Signs-From-Heaven Stuffing – When situations seem coincidental, yet are so profound…you know you are receiving confirmation from above. The message is clear, grabs you by the tail, and fires up your spirit.

How-to Guide for Piñatas – The life manual that you did not get at birth nor was it given to you at school. This guide would have saved a lot of bumps to your noggin along the way, made you wiser and helped you navigate through real-life. Have no fear, *The Piñata Theory™* is here. Because you are a newcomer to earth and human, accept that you had some cranky stuffing along the way. Rejoice in your inherent ability to evolve and *Step into Your Greatness*.

Step into Your Greatness – Becoming, and stepping into, your God-given authentic self. Living your life through the heart of your existence — spirit. Embracing your inner voice, a seed of greatness planted by God. This brilliance within, guides you to become more like Him, by continually thriving to be the best version of you — aligning with your life purpose, sharing your gifts, love, intelligence, and beautiful stuffing with the world. Your journey here is to serve and honor God.

Human Piñata – A human being. A human being what? Hopefully, the best Piñata you can be!

Piñata Top 10 - Life Lessons List – Write down the top life lessons you learned each year in a journal. Be honest and insightful. As you move forward in life, review and acknowledge the great progress and discoveries you have made. Celebrate your victories, lessons, awareness and growth. Your top life lessons can include recognizing your achievements and personal transformation, such as a new lifestyle, learned skills, and *Pinata Ah-Ha Moments.*

Heavy-Piñata-Wagon – A way to get you to stop thinking about people or hurtful things that happened in the past. Envision yourself pulling a wagon with you, everywhere you go. This wagon is full of Piñata Poop — the crap and people you won't let go of. Now, stop and reflect on this image. Do you really want to pull that heaviness around with you every day? Let go of that wagon my dear Piñata. It serves no healthy or productive role in your life. Use my *Heavy-Piñata-Wagon* example, when you begin to think of a person who hurt you. See them sitting in a wagon full of Piñata Poop, following you everywhere. Stop smiling, this is serious.

Sparkling Piñata Tips

Throughout this book, I provide life tips that will make your exterior shell shine and your stuffing all warm and fuzzy.

It is my hope these sparkles bring you back in time, to a place of innocence, discovery, self-actualization and love.

You will gather new, positive, scrumptious, loving and healthy stuffing.

You are what you digest after all — mind, body and spirit.

The Piñata Theory™
Table of Contents

The Piñata Theory™

What's in your Stuffing?

by Charlene Renaud

Chapter One
A Symbolic Theory About You and a Piñata

What does a Piñata have to do with what's stuffed inside you?

A Piñata is a colorful animal (or another shape), made of papier-mache. Anxious and excited children line up at birthday parties, waiting for someone to tie a blindfold around their head and hand them a stick. After they are spun in circles, they strike wildly at the air until stick meets Piñata, releasing a burst of candy and small toys hidden inside. The lucky whack spills all of the delicious candy and trinkets onto the floor, while the children scatter like mice to pick up every piece. It's paradise in a paper donkey, and lots of fun.

What drives a child to beat a paper animal, a/k/a Piñata? Is it to express their anger or frustration? No. They want candy. Just as Cookie Monster exhibits enthusiasm over cookies — children are passionate about their candy. It's not healthy for children to max out on excess candy. Yet dabbling in a few *M&M's®, Smarties®*, or *Tootsie Rolls®* every once in a while, will please their sweet tooth and soothe their souls.

Where does a child's desire to burst open a Piñata for candy come from?

The child's data bank (their subconscious mind), was downloaded with the data (information), that you can beat a Piñata, bust it open and discover a candy reward. This data came from a person I refer to as a downloader — such as a teacher, parent, caregiver, a relative or a friend. This experience is stored in the child's subconscious mind as: candy is good. It is a prize or a reward.

The inside of a Piñata is stuffed with goodies, and in order to get the gems, one must burst it open. In this way, Piñatas and people have much in common.

Think of yourself as a Piñata and ask yourself, *What's stuffed inside of me?*

From conception, you have been stuffed or downloaded with masses of information, beliefs, pictures, experiences and so on. All of your stuffing is stored in your data bank.

In order to crack your *Piñata Code™*, you need to look at what you were stuffed with by examining what has been downloaded. Determine if it is good stuffing, bad stuffing, factual stuffing, silly stuffing, family dynamic stuffing, cultural stuffing, self-image stuffing, (un) healthy stuffing, religious stuffing and so forth.

When you came into the world and during your formative years, you had no control over most of what you downloaded — others stuffed your young mind. You were a *Baby Piñata* with no filter and you naturally absorbed everything.

What's stuffed inside of you? Why does it matter? This is what I'd like to tickle you with in this chapter. Your past life experiences (your ethnicity, religious or spiritual beliefs, your address on the planet, your family life, your education, traumatic events, relationships) are stored like data inside your Piñata's subconscious mind.

This stuffing, or hidden data, powerfully influences every moment of your life today. It can be damaging and paralyzing like kryptonite to Superman, or transforming and life changing like an Olympic medal to an athlete. Your stuff affects your automatic responses, emotions, and decisions.

But, what if you could consciously sift through the layers of stuffing in your Piñata's data bank and select what's in your best immediate and long-term interests?

- Do you have the conscious power and ability to do that?
- Do you have the ability to override or diminish the effects of destructive stuffing?
- Can you put more stuffing in your Piñata?

Yes, yes, yes. Absolutely!

How do I know so much about stuffing?

I'm not a doctor. I do not have a University degree. I'm not a Certified, Board Sanctioned Stuffologist. Nor did I work in a toy factory stuffing colorful paper animals with white puffy material and bon-bons. I earned a Master's in Life Experience, especially when it came to bursting open, (often painfully), my Piñata or subconscious mind.

Through my personal experience, I had a lot of unhealthy stuffing that needed examination and dissection, in order to figure out why I made some of the automatic, unconscious decisions that I'd made. I compassionately began to see and understand that I was extracting solely from my old pre-loaded stuffing.

When I began, it took a lot of effort to pick and sort that stuffing out. It involved diving head-first into my subconscious data bank. Some of the stuff I had stored inside of me had sat in the dark for a long time and it hurt coming out. Some of my saved memories made me smile. Other parts of the stuff in that vast data bank made me laugh. There were things I wished I could forget or wipe from my memory. Parts of my stuffing made me wonder, *What was I thinking*?

My conclusion? I wasn't thinking. The stuffing in my subconscious mind rattled often, and periodically made uncomfortable noises, making me wonder if I would ever feel real peace. My subconscious mind drove the bus and I sat in the back seat, wondering when the bumpy ride was going to end.

The knowledge and information I am writing in this book is derived from my own experiences about how my stuffing affected my life, as well as observations from the lives of others. In my twenty-two years filling a policing role, I have witnessed vast differences in people's perceptions, beliefs, lifestyles, health, challenges and expectations. In addition, as a singer, I have had the opportunity to meet hundreds of people — and all of these experiences drive me to question. *Why are all people different?*

The answer I've discovered, is because, no two Piñatas are stuffed the same. Yet, we have many commonalities that we experience as humans: pain, joy, love, disappointment, excitement and so on.

I also work through the inner voice that speaks to me and through me, to help others see clearly. These are the kinds of investigative questions that help me filter through stuffing to find the facts:

- What do you believe and accept, and why?
- What do you have the ability to change?
- Why is every human responsible for stopping the destruction of self and others? (i.e., relationships, animals, the planet)
- How do you have the best life possible, regardless of your past, through the power of conscious thinking?
- Why are your thoughts pure energy that determine your future?
- How important is it to load your mind and data bank with great stuffing?
- Do you realize that you have magical stuffing inside of you called your spirit? Did you know your spirit is connected to the most powerful force in the universe?
- Did you know that communicating with, seeking knowledge and direction from, trusting and believing in a divine source (God, Creator, a Higher Power, or a Universal Source) will enrich your life with joy, peace and gratefulness?

Further in the book, I am going to unveil *The Piñata Code™*, the key to achieving greatness. You will discover your hidden gems, share them and live your authentic *Piñata Purpose*. This may influence you to protect your Piñata from acquiring *Sheep Piñata Syndrome* — eating up everything that you see and hear in the media, on the street and the internet. *Sheep Piñatas* are followers and go along with the crowd. This book is for those who are demoralized by the damaging effect of greed, control, materialism, racism and radicalism — all destructive to mankind, animals and the planet.

Why do some Piñatas clearly see these global problems as being a detriment, yet others could care less or even contribute to it? Through a conscious mind shift you will become consciously aware of the human created data that you have digested. It is then your choice to accept it as truth or as common stuffing that *Sheep Piñatas* feed off of and *believe*.

Sheep Piñatas are grazers and behave like zombies in *The Walking Dead*, wandering through life aimlessly and without purpose. Grazers are not concerned about what they digest, just as long as they are fed. Burp! Their bellies are sore and they develop ulcers from toxic and harmful stuff.

Then there are the *Piñata Sheep Herders* — those with a purpose, a knowing and a desire to share their gifts and talents with the world, to make it a better place. They also consume human knowledge, sometimes inventing new concepts and theories themselves. But, *Piñata Sheep Herders* differ in nature, as leaders who won't feed on just anything, and are careful about what they ingest into their bodies. They have a high level of intelligence, beyond book smarts, and know there is more than what we see, hear, smell and touch.

A key element of a *Piñata Sheep Herder* is that they rely heavily on instinct and depend on a Higher Source of being to direct them. The *Piñata Sheep Herder's* spirit is alive, thriving and wants to live the way the higher power intended them to live. The *Sheep Herder* applies the teachings from a non-human source: God, The Source, a Higher Power, The Divine, or a Universal Power. For simplicity, I personally refer to this Higher Power as God in the book. Your upbringing, influences, culture, language and state of existence all intertwine to identify an entity that resonates with you, which is a non-human source. This entity is not seen, though real. When a person connects with this Source, life changes dramatically for the better.

What does this mean to you?

Although we live in a human world, you and I are gifted with a spirit, which is separate from the conscious and subconscious mind. The spirit has no ego-based human stuffing: fearful, flawed and limited. Your spirit is pure and connected to a Divine Source that is made up of truth and love and unlimited potential. The spirit within is a natural knowing that speaks to us. Some call it their inner voice, gut feeling or intuition. In order to live a spirit-filled existence; one must acknowledge the spirit within, and trust in God to provide flawless life-changing stuffing.

Our spirit is the seed of truth and wisdom that is planted within us, in every cell of life, from a Source that is powerful beyond measure. The origin of our spirit comes from God. He is the Master Planner, the All-Mighty and the All-Knowing. God is the source of love, forgiveness and miracles. God made all that is in the universe and He has a divine plan for your life. Once you accept Him, learn more about Him, praise Him, thank and protect Mother Earth, and follow His teaching, the richer your life will be. You will become a Sheep Herder, leading others to a new way of living.

Our spirit is also aware that there is something more beyond things, money, titles or ego and can see and feel deeply, the crash of humanity and the planet all around us. Most of us can feel the effects of terrorism, war, and global warming, to the degree that the pending destruction of mankind, the animal kingdom, and Mother Earth herself, appear imminent.

I've always felt the spirit within, yet I was filled primarily with *Human Stuffing* that was stored in my Piñata's hard drive, making me behave like a sheep instead of a *Piñata Sheep Herder*. I had spirit-filled moments in my life, including revelations and miracles, yet I remained trapped in my own mind, drawing information and direction from my subconscious data bank. I had no idea that my subconscious mind — my stuffing — had such a powerful impact on my life.

My stuff was buried beneath the surface of what I could see, hear and smell. After purposely reading countless self-help and wellness books, and with the help of an incredible psychologist, Manny, I dug up old bones and also discovered hidden treasures in my stuffing. I discovered that I was made of pure gold.

I learned I was a spiritual being created by God. My shell, my Piñata, was the house of my spirit. Yet, through time, lots of worthless scrap was stuffed inside of me, weighing me down and limiting my potential. I won't spill all the delicious jelly beans right now, but as you turn the pages, I'll reveal how these discoveries dramatically changed *my life*. These gems will enrich your Piñata, better than candy stuffing. As you continue to read, I will inspire you to believe in yourself, see your unlimited potential, love yourself and show you just how special and unique you are. You were designed to be a mirror image of The Divine and you were formed by the hand of God. There is no other Piñata, just like you.

In the following pages, you will learn how to celebrate life to its fullest. I will show you how your stuffing has affected you. You will say bah-bye to your garbage stuffing and put it out with the trash. With intent, you can make the power of your subconscious mind work for you by pounding the old negative stuffing out of your Piñata, making room for more of the delectable delights that will sweeten your purpose.

Chapter Two
Purging Your Piñata Poop (Toxic Stuffing)

In order to enjoy a happier and healthier life, you need to be consciously aware of the impact of, and, what's been stuffed (or stored), inside your data bank — the subconscious mind. In doing so, one can then understand how their stuffing impacts daily responses, behavior, health and potential. Like a child with a stick hitting a Piñata, this book will give you the code and handy tools to open your data bank of stuffing. You will discover the hidden treasures that help you, and the toxic stuffing that is harmful or unhealthy for you. Armed with this *Piñata Decoder*, you will be able to separate truth from myth and dramatically change your life for the better.

The candy (or data) stuffed inside your Piñata, will remain status quo until you consciously choose to accept it as being healthy or unhealthy. Further, if you continue to stuff your *Precious Piñata* with unhealthy, false or harmful data, don't expect better outcomes. If a person chooses to eat too much candy, then one must accept the outcome of doing so. A person who eats lots of candy, will eventually get a belly ache or develop diabetes or become overweight, all of which lead to health problems.

Turn the page to discover a new *Sparkling Piñata Tip* to download into your Personal Piñata!

Throughout this book, I will refer to the stuffing in your Piñata as the data in your subconscious mind. Your Piñata (pick any animal or shape you'd like), holds a huge memory bank of everything you've ever seen, experienced, heard and learned. It's like a mega hard-drive containing your life. There is so much information stored in your subconscious mind, that no computer on earth has enough space to store it all.

Really? You bet your sweet Piñata bonbons!

How big *is* your subconscious mind? Can this stuffing or memory within your Piñata be measured?

No, that is impossible. It's infinite, as it includes not only your life experiences, it also contains cultural beliefs and all of the data down-loaded into your *Baby Piñata* from your *Parent Piñata's* DNA. Your DNA contains links to the past and to your ancestry. These genetic memories are embedded within your cells.

Your DNA is also wired to help you stay alive. It contains your basic *Piñata Survival Instinct* — your built-in, automatic defense system. This helps you survive under extreme duress or when facing a life-threatening situation, by creating chemical reactions in the body.

Is it possible that your DNA also contains feelings, emotions and experiences from our ancestors? Can you imagine reliving what someone experienced a century ago? What if that experience was cultural genocide?

Consider the pain felt by *First Nations*, (their family and community), a group forced into residential schools in Canada under the direction of Her Majesty the Queen. I believe this cultural pain is passed through generations, via DNA, and subconsciously affects millions of people today. However, to be released from pain, one must choose to end suffering. It is unnecessary and unhealthy to continually live in a state of victimhood.

How can we tap into centuries of data planted as a code within our DNA? Our conscious mind does not have the ability to do that. However, our subconscious mind or dream state has the ability to access this information. This is what I refer to as the *Sub-Piñata State* — being in a dream state, functioning within the subconscious mind. When you sleep, your conscious mind shuts down and your subconscious mind remains awake. Actually, the subconscious mind never sleeps. It runs 24/7.

Another way to get inside the *Sub-Piñata State* is to meditate — turning off your conscious mind and floating into the unknown. Think of consciousness as being awake, aware and the now. The subconscious like a fine veil, once opened, is the doorway to the past. How far back, we will never know. Hypnosis is also a mechanism used to access and communicate with the subconscious mind.

It is believed that the subconscious mind is thousands of times more powerful than the conscious mind. When you factor in DNA that contains an infinite amount of information, this number is incomprehensible. There is no measuring tool that could give us an exact number, as no human has completely accessed every grain of life that was passed to or experienced by them.

The Grand Illusion Stuffing

All of that which is in our subconscious mind came from somewhere. As a whole, a significant portion of where you are today, is based on what's happened in your life, between your date of birth and now.

Everyone is in the same boat so to speak, meaning our stuffing is relevant to our generation. In 100 years, if humanity still exists, that world will look back at our world and will probably be disgusted to discover that the main goal of a large number of humans was to get rich and to collect more possessions, at all costs.

Sadly, today's world is full of selfish, self-gratifying and self-centered Piñatas.

It is my hope that the next century of humans will be much smarter, improving where we have failed. Think about the lyrics to Bette Midler's song, *From a Distance*. "*God is watching us, God is watching us,*" and "*There are no guns, no bombs and no disease, no hungry mouths to feed.*" This would be a perfect world.

The fallout of a materialist world is guns, bombs, disease, poverty and all things unfair and ugly. We were not created to love stuff. We were created to love self, others, animals, the Earth and mostly, God. We were created to share, to help, to give, to praise and be plentiful in spirit, with the focus on the wellness of family, community and love.

Gluttony has led to a vast depletion of habitat, and a mind that focuses on things, versus universal wellness or people. The bigger, better, faster, newer machine-lifestyle is being loaded into the subconscious mind, where later, the unsuspecting human will draw and feed upon its poison. Like drinking from an infected watering hole or receiving a tainted injection, we unknowingly fill ourselves with toxins.

The cycle of more things, becomes an addiction of sorts, because the fuel is coming from a source that supports the need for more, to be more. We are becoming dependent on machines for answers to questions, devices that perform tasks for us, such as *Siri*, *Google Home* and *Amazon Echo*. Addiction to things destroys the spirit and more is never enough.

I've been guilty of this. In the past, if I really wanted something, I bought it. I thought my purchases would satisfy me. Yet, I still felt unfulfilled. I needed more, another thing, or to do this or that. In this kind of state, the fix of getting, achieving or feeling satisfied becomes harder and harder to quench. More things are then needed to become satisfied, to transcend the Piñata into a space of bullshit and a virtual escape from reality. This repetitive behavior never satisfies the hunger of the spirit to live a life centered on truth and love.

If it only takes money and fame to be happy, then why do so many rich and famous celebrities fall prey to drug addiction, cheating on spouses, depression and even suicide?

The celebrity, artist or musician shares a gift or talent freely or as a paid profession. They are the people who entertain us through music, movies, TV shows, radio shows and stage performances. These talents or gifts are implanted within one's spirit, within a carrier (a human being) to be used to help, inspire, teach, worship (God) and celebrate life moments.

When the use of the gift or talent is shifted from the spiritual component (to enrich) to the fixation of fame and money, then the whole purpose of the gift is sacrificed and unhappiness results. The gift is then exploited and a shift takes place from the love of creating, for a higher purpose, to feeding one's ego to become famous, rich and having more stuff. I am not saying that artists shouldn't be paid, they absolutely deserve every penny and there are many starving artists. What I am stating is, pay should not be the driving force for the artist, *the beauty of creativity* must be paramount.

The ego feeds off of the type of stuffing that makes us believe that people with more money are living the dream. Just watch a lottery commercial on TV. Winning millions is going to be the ticket to freedom and happiness. This image of bliss has been downloaded into our Piñata. In actuality, few people strike it rich in the lottery.

A belief system is thus created, suggesting that having more stuff equals happiness. In order to have more stuff, a person needs to work longer hours (generally speaking), sacrificing time with family and friends.

I call this person the *More-Stuff-Piñata* (MSP). This Piñata spends so much time working, that they are missing the whole point of *living*. The *More-Stuff-Piñata* believes that happiness comes from collecting stuff. But, what the MSP hasn't thought through, is that all this stuff costs more money to have, to maintain, to insure, to clean, to fix.

The MSP also feels important showing their stuff to other Piñatas. They wish to impress other Piñatas with their possessions. This spirit-poor Piñata lives to make more money to buy more stuff, yet is truly not happy in the end.

They wake up one day and kick themselves in the Piñata butt for not focusing on *what matters most in life*: their children, mate, time, and enjoying things that are peaceful and enjoyable to them. This could be faith, walking in the forest, fishing or watching a sunset on the beach. Priceless, my Piñatas.

If you feel you have some of the traits of a More-Stuff-Piñata, please help yourself to some delicious new stuffing:

- Money doesn't make you happy. If you need a gold toilet seat to feel important, you are missing the point of life. Your Piñata's behind won't care either.

- Reconnect with nature by walking through a park or forest and feel the new energy it gives you. Lie in the grass and look up at the sky. Feel the blades of grass between your toes. Take a drive up to the mountains and breathe in the spectacular view and air. Go to a nursery and buy yourself some plants or trees and go play in the dirt.

- Work where you enjoy working, using your best talents and skills. Don't focus solely on income as a way to define your choices in employment.

- If you hate your job, but love the money, you are going to lose something in the end. Your spirit knows the truth and eventually you may experience loss in health, happiness, creativity, and relationships.

- Choose a rich spirit first: be grateful for life, for nature, for God. Be thankful for food, clothing, shelter, life, family and healthy relationships.

- Ask yourself daily, what can I do to make the world a better place? Come up with small or big gesture and act on it.

- When a Piñata is about to cross over to the spirit world, do you honestly think that they are concerned about what they accumulated in their life? I'd rather be thinking about how I treated people, how I made the world a better place, and the relationships that mattered most to me.

- You enjoy the same air, same moon and sun as the richest people in the world. These are free and God's gift to us.

- Make a point of examining your motives and focus. Do you buy stuff so that people will like you? Do you buy stuff to impress others? Do you need all that stuff? I've seen people buy friend-ships. These never last.

- Spend less money, give more to others. Donate time and money to community needs.

- Challenge yourself to stop doing routine things over and over. Shake life up a bit by stepping out of your comfort zone and try something fun and new. Go out to a karaoke show, take up a running class, join a theatre group, or do anything out of the ordinary for *you*.

- Stop gifting people who have so much stuff. Many holidays and celebrations are traditional times that we give things to others — to people who have lots of material possessions. I suggest using all of the gift money to buy groceries for a food bank, donate it to a community group or to cancer research, or helping a child in an impoverished area acquire food, shelter and education. Think of a cause you would like to support and do it. Send a card to your beloved and tell them how their gift is changing someone's life.

Instructions for Purging Piñata Poop

Relax and think for about 15-20 minutes, about what's stuffed inside of you, where it came from, from who and how long it has been there and how it is affecting you today – good or bad.

Take a note pad and write down the positive and negative stuffing that you consumed, inhaled, heard, experienced or seen.

Now, consciously prepare your Piñata to purge your *Piñata Poop* — this is unhealthy toxic stuffing that hurts you.

See yourself putting all of this toxic stuffing inside personalized cans, labelled, "My Piñata Poop." Take the cans and line them up on a fence.

Place your Piñata in *Dwayne Johnson (The Rock)* shoes. He is one hardcore, *Bad-Ass Piñata.* Think about what *The Rock* said about hard times, "*I like to use the hard times in the past to motivate me today.*"

Now see your Piñata carrying a *Super-High-Powered-Piñata-Poop-Popper.* As you bring your weapon up, to align the scope with your eyes, focus on the cans that are loaded with trouble.

When you unload, *unload*. Say out loud: pop, pop, pop, pop, pop. Hear the sound ringing in your ears. You terminate the cans like *The Terminator*; they blow up into smithereens and fly into the universe a million miles away.

You feel light, relieved and delivered of heavy *GMO*-laden *Piñata Poop* that has held you down for many moons. There's so many toxins in that stuff, no wonder, you were feeling heavy!

Throughout the book you will discover the importance of loading healthy new stuffing and how to keep it.

Congratulations, You Bad-Ass Piñata!

Chapter Three
The Piñata Theory™ is Born _ The Subconscious Mind & Unhealthy Stuffing

The Piñata Theory™ came to me when speaking to my marketing assistant and friend, Tracy Lamourie. We were discussing promotional projects and she asked me how life was going.

I said, "I went through hell to get to heaven," referring to a recent toxic relationship. "Thankfully, God, faith, friends and family helped me climb back from a very dark, deep and painful place. I had hit rock bottom in my life and swore I would never live through that experience again." I added, "But, I acquired valuable insight about my life by bursting open my subconscious like bursting open a Piñata."

"I love that analogy," Tracy said. "You are definitely here to teach others."

It was a major *Piñata Ah-ha* moment for me. From that second, I knew this statement would became my legacy and a metaphorical conduit to teach others. *The Piñata Theory™* was born.

The hell I referred to when talking with Tracy, came from a damaging relationship, and quite frankly, years of unhealthy relationships that compiled one after another. In a sense, I had to burst myself open to figure out why I chose the type of mates that I did.

I needed to put an end to the roller coaster of suffering caused by toxic, drama-injected relationships. In order to do so, I needed to dig deeply into the core of my being: my values, beliefs, triggers, patterns and layers of stuff, stored in my subconscious mind. I worked with many counselors who helped me dig up old bones uncovering self-defeating stuffing. All of them offered very helpful insights, advice and resources to help in my journey. Each of them helped me see my weaknesses and my strengths.

I urge you to consider professional counseling if you are feeling lost, uncertain, stuck, depressed, sad or afraid. You may be holding on to painful stuffing and no matter what it is, you will benefit immensely by purging it and dealing with it with the help of a professional. Taking the first step may be scary, but in time, your life will be clearer. If I can help through Life Coaching – information can be found at the end of this book.

I started seeing counselors and doctors in my twenties. My family doctor suggested I join *Al-Anon*, since I'm a child of an alcoholic father. He knew about my family dynamics stuffing, being the sole practitioner for my parents and siblings.

We lived in a small rural community, so everyone knew everyone's business, including what was happening at our house — the local watering hole at the time. Dr. Piñata's reason for suggesting *Al-Anon* was to help me open up my Piñata, to see how alcoholism affected me in many ways. He suggested *Al-Anon* might allow me to see the impact of someone else's drinking on my life.

Alcoholism is a family illness as it affects every relative in different ways. Without the valuable tool of *Al-Anon*, I was not equipped or stuffed with the knowledge I needed to protect myself. I was left vulnerable, and chose persons with dysfunctional lives. Little did I know then, that for the next thirty years I would become *co-dependent,* living as sick as those I tried to fix.

Looking back now, I would have benefited greatly by joining *Al-Anon*. I would have saved myself a lot of misery. For years, I justified my avoidance for help and support. I couldn't understand why I needed to attend meetings about living with an alcoholic. I told myself, *I'm not the alcoholic. I'm not the one who needs fixing.*

Since birth, I was trained to accept alcohol as a part of life — as normal and essential as water. I stuffed myself with alcohol, as this was the normal, acceptable behavior in my family. I was like my tribal Piñatas — often consuming alcohol to the point of intoxication or to the point of getting sick. Depending on the drink and the level of my consumption, I acted out in silly, stupid, funny, careless, risky or cranky ways. I can remember falling on a bed trying to stop the head spins. For me, drinking was simply a part of life — it was part of my routine.

Yet, something inside of me was telling me that this lifestyle was not right. Consuming alcohol was beginning to feel destructive and unnecessary. That inner voice began to tell me I was not created to abuse myself, and doing so was in opposition to love.

Self-love was not part of my upbringing or makeup. My background conditioned me to put others ahead of my own welfare and needs. I always felt I needed to do something (sex, drinking, drugs, buying things, being in the club) to earn love. My self-esteem was severely damaged — I had no concept of dignity.

Maybe you can relate to my mixed up normal. Does this resonate with you or someone you know?

Love starts with self — first through connection with spirit and with God. I know this now, but as you'll discover in the next chapter, my story spiraled down before I learned how to move my mind up.

Chapter Four

The Fall of My Piñata: When the Paper Walls Came Crashing Down

In February 2012, during my third marriage to a man named Jack, I suffered a psychogenic stress reaction. It resulted in handcuffs, jail and domestic charges. I literally had a mental breakdown. My mind and body told me, *No more. I'm finished.*

My *Piñata Survival Instinct* took over.

My mind literally went into survival mode, after years of mental abuse and lies from Jack and his well-trained offspring. His children's stuffing was sadly mixed with their father's stuffing, and it was toxic. He taught his kids unhealthy dysfunction about how to treat women — which was not respectful, loving, or kind.

To this day, I believe their mother should have ran as far as she could go with her children, to get away from that man. I believe she'd still be alive today, and her daughters would have had a chance at normalcy. She committed suicide by drinking *Drano* and a cocktail of chemicals. My heart aches every time I think of her.

When I met Jack, and walked into his house for the first time, I thought, *This place could be on the show Hoarders.*

The nine-year-old daughter's bedroom door had the words: *slut, kill* and *whore,* spray painted across the front of the door that faced the hallway.

Claw marks scraped past the paint and dug into the wood of the door. The marks ran vertically down the front of the door. I felt like I was standing on the set of a horror movie.

Healthy-minded women would have said, "Gee, I have to go," and made up any excuse to get out of that place. However, I was more interested in fixing.

All I could think was, *These poor kids. I can fix this and Jack will appreciate me.*

I would be his savior, doing the tasks that he had no care to do, including trying to get him to discipline his children.

That was like taming wild cats. They were well beyond the influential stage and contained stuffing that was full of selfishness, deception and a "do what you need to do in order to survive mentality." They no doubt, had developed coping and survival mechanisms to survive in a very dysfunctional home. They did not choose this situation, it was thrust upon them. But the consequences were all theirs.

I had my own consequences to contend with. My arrest was shocking to all who knew me, as many referred to me as an *angel*. This incident was totally out of character.

I was well-known and respected for doing a lot of work in the community through my music and volunteer work. In my job as a Special Constable at the local police service, I spearheaded drug addiction and drug education projects that affected the lives of many people in a positive way, mostly youth.

I had a solid reputation. I was known for helping others, not hurting them.

A few months prior to my traumatic breakdown, many things were happening, warning me of my pending mental collapse.

Firstly, my body was screaming from the pain of fibromyalgia resulting from stress. I walked like I was a frail old woman. My body was clearly telling me that my environment was horrid. Yet, I continued to do it all, attempting to feed my approval addiction.

I was determined to stick it out, because I couldn't deal with the embarrassment of another failed marriage. I felt I'd never live that one down, especially since I felt shamed by a couple of siblings, with each relationship failure.

I have lived with trauma for most of my life. My stuffing marked me with many painful memories. Once, a relative chased me with a shovel in a rage, one night when he was totally drunk. For a reason I never figured out, he was pissed off at me. Thankfully, his friend Paul, was present. Paul was a gentle giant who held him down and stopped him from attacking me. Otherwise, I would have been seriously injured or perhaps dead.

Deep down, I knew I did not belong in those situations. I had a special purpose and God was going to show me the way out of misery. God tried to get through to me for years. I brushed him off. I believed in him, but had no idea his love for me ran so deep, and that he wanted to show me a healthy, loving, spiritual and beautiful life.

I was a chronic co-dependent and Jack's troubles were a natural fit for me. I was drawn to the drama, fixing and instability. I was abused over and over, yet covered the truth by creating a false reality.

In spite of signs, flags, and encouragement from many people to abandon this relationship, I stayed. My friend Karen said, "Don't walk Charlene, run."

I was unclear as to what a healthy relationship represented to me. I witnessed healthy relationships that others had and wanted the same, yet, my stuffing was distorted.

If you are a damaged Piñata, you will cling to and hang around (no pun intended) other damaged Piñatas.

I received many intuitive gut feelings that things were not right. I justified reality by telling myself, *Jack loves me and needs me.*

You may feel something inside of you when you read the last sentence. Do you try and fix others at your own expense? Do you feel it your responsibility to care for people who won't even care for themselves? Are you desperate to be loved, at all costs? Or are you the opposite?

A Piñata with healthy self-esteem can recognize unhealthy situations and knows how to protect their shell and stuffing!

If you are a chronic fixer or giver, it's time to work on your own Piñata and understand your past influences and choices, so you can carve a new reality for yourself starting today. When this epiphany first came to me, I couldn't have imagined the dramatic way it would arrive. November 11, 2011, (11/11/11), was the day the angels came. I'm not kidding.

On that day, I was married to Jack, and in hindsight, I think the angels must have been desperate to get through to me. That evening, I was sleeping in bed and was awakened by a beautiful, bright, white light in the bedroom.

My first thought was that a helicopter was landing outside, yet the light was centered in the room. I was trying to justify what I was seeing, glancing to where my laptop was. It was closed and dark.

The light was so bright, it was like super-charged LED, times a hundred-fold. Oddly, I didn't feel afraid, as the light's glow felt peaceful. I feel back to sleep.

The next day, after seeing the light, I contacted two angel therapy practitioners who I'd met, previously. One said I needed protection, and the other said, "A woman who took her life in her early forties has come to settle the score with her husband and children."

Ironically, Jack's ex-wife was in her forties when she took her life. Chills shimmied down my spine as her eerie message hit home.

Around the same time frame, the stereo and lights began to turn on by themselves, at all hours, while people slept. Music that shouldn't have played started waking me anywhere from 2:00 a.m. to 4:00 a.m.

I learned through this experience, the universe, angels, and your guides, will send you warnings and lifelines. Pay attention to these Mayday messages from the heavens!

My Broken Piñata

In early 2012, my Piñata stopped. All of my efforts to fix came to an end, and I was now the one who needed fixing. I was broken — but something positive came from it. It took the life-changing event of reaching my own end, for me to leave a very toxic relationship.

My son Jordan said it best, "Mom, had this not of happened, you'd still be there, trying to fix them."

He was right. The end of this relationship saved my life.

Like a stack of cards, one fell at a time, then the whole deck crashed. The signs of the pending fall had started months before and finally came to a head.

I remember having a horrible sick feeling. It seemed I was surrounded by overwhelming negativity when my daughter Lisa left to go to school in New York. It was me, left with Jack and his three children. It felt like the wolves were moving in for the kill. They had me outnumbered, with no witnesses.

The *angel* had met the *devil* and his true colors emerged. I quickly gained a better understanding as to why Jack's last wife continually pleaded for help — and what happened to her in the end.

When she died, the police and fire department attended the apartment Jack's wife lived in, as her body was removed. An officer told me that it was the worst suicide they had ever seen. This once vibrant, educated, beautiful woman went through horrific pain in the last moments of her life.

As the officer described the scene, I couldn't help realizing how easily something like that could have happened to me. I suffered a psychosis which ironically *saved my life*. There is no coincidence that both she and I experienced similar events.

Jack once told me, referring to his ex-wife, "I didn't know what to do, so I did nothing. After all, it was her who wanted those children, not me."

The Strangers Call

After the fallout, I received a message from a complete stranger. Bill (not his real name), said he knew Jack's ex-wife. He heard what happened to me and wanted to talk. At first, I was afraid and thought Jack or his kids were up to no good. Feeling cautious, I agreed to meet him in a public place.

We sat in a local restaurant where he pulled papers from a briefcase. He laid them out carefully on the table in front of us. These, he said, pointing at the papers on the table, were about me — public credentials about my life work that he researched on the internet.

He said, "How could someone like this, have done that?" He was referring to the domestic charges concocted against me. He said, "I believe in you, Charlene."

He proceeded to say that Jack's ex-wife confided in him. She told Bill that she was abused by Jack and her oldest son. One of them had pushed her down a flight of stairs at home and kicked her out. Another time, she was left at an airport, while Jack remained on a boarded plane. She said Jack locked her in a room and told her she was crazy.

Jack's ex-wife eventually became bipolar and schizophrenic. Bill looked at me as tears poured down his face and said, "I wish I could have saved her." He never imagined she would take her life.

When I first met Jack, he told me his ex-wife claimed he abused cocaine, but that it was not factual. However, a few months after my breakdown, I was told by someone else that Jack was snorting cocaine long before I met him. This explained why he often sniffled and complained of a runny nose when I first met him. The truth was coming out. Painfully.

The more I learned, the more I cringed, knowing I slept with him. I was in bed with the enemy. My background caused me to trust too much and love for all the wrong reasons, having no idea that such evil existed. And yet, there were more pieces to unearth in my Piñata's stuffing. As I'll share next, some of my wrappings looked sweet, but didn't necessarily contain good things.

Chapter Five
The Over-Giving and Over-Forgiving Piñata

The more I came to terms with myself, my conditioning and perceptions, my reality, a question burned in my mind.

How could I have put myself through this pain, disgrace and aggravation?

The answer was right there in my history. Because, a portion of my childhood stuffing taught me to:

- Put up and shut up
- Internalize my feelings
- Work hard physically to gain approval
- Take on others responsibilities when they are not responsible
- Keep the peace
- Be a doormat
- Create a false reality to conceal the truth

Why did I not worry about my well-being as much as pleasing others? Because I had no concept of self-care or self-respect. I believed it was selfish to think of myself and to do what was healthy for me.

Further, my Catholic upbringing engrained in me, like a tattoo, to forgive others. No one explained *the fine print* about abusive relationships, self-care, and protection.

I was never taught that it's necessary to protect yourself against mental, emotional or physical abuse. I was never told I had the birthright to be respected, valued, and loved. I also had the right to be happy, healthy, to dream and be fully deserving of a wonderful life instead of feeling obliged to remain in a toxic relationship.

At that time, the stuffing downloaded into my Piñata was to forgive. I never received full disclosure — if a person mistreats you over and over, then you must stand up for yourself and do what is best for you.

I broke up with Jack several times before we married. Yet, I'd forgive him. He said he would change. It was a cycle of repetitious behavior and dysfunction and I was the only one trying. Like a broken record, we were stuck, repeating the same song. There were plenty of warning signs, yet I avoided the blatant truth and continued in the relationship for a time, further harming myself, instead of healing.

Think about situations in your life. Are you being honest? Do you feel respected, valued and loved? Do you protect, love and nurture yourself?

It is your responsibility to take care of your Piñata.

Childhood stuffing has a substantial and direct influence on a Piñata's life experience. Your parents and mine, received their stuffing from their parents. Much of what our parents taught us, was reflective of the belief systems, in the generation they were born in. *Generational Stuffing* is stuffing based on the knowledge-of-the-day within a generation of people born at specific times.

Generational Stuffing

In my parent's generation, (post world war II) many women worked at home in a traditional role, limiting opportunities available to them outside of their own four walls. The role of a stay-at-home-mother or home-maker, didn't generally have the same respect, value or leverage of a man's role outside of the home.

Television shows in that time glorified women in an apron. They ran to the door to greet their man with a welcome kiss, as their mate after all, had a hard day. The man earned money — he put the bread and butter on the table.

Women worked very hard as well — doing laundry, cleaning, cooking, and rearing children. Women generally did not receive the praise they deserved and were not encouraged to work elsewhere. However, there were a few rare men who encouraged their partners to pursue their dreams and praised them for their hard work at home. Women in this era who did work outside the home, were commonly secretaries, teachers, and nurses.

For the most part, men living in the traditional generation spent less time with their children, as it was largely a female role to mind the *Piñata Cubs*.

During the following baby-boomer generation, a shift began for women. They stayed at home, or built a career, or tried to have it all — a blend of career and family. Their male mates were mentored by the previous generation, to be mainly the breadwinner, not a caregiver. The imbalance of home and child responsibilities with two working parents began. Women juggled children, home and work. Masculine structures were still mainly observed and honored. More women began to enroll in advanced education and were stepping into formerly dominant male roles — lawyers, police officers, doctors to name a few.

Fast track to the tail end of the baby boomers and the beginning of Generation X. People of this era grew up with career parents and the shifting of male dominant structures. Many Gen X partners equally share raising children and caring for the home. This generation is less about hierarchy and structure and more about relationships and experiences. Many people born in this generation also experienced growing up in divorced families, going to day care and being latch-key kids. This generation has a high percentage of educated people who had many options in careers to choose from.

Social evolution continues to change in Gen Y. This generation is technologically advanced, sophisticated about life due to their exposure to expanding media platforms and the internet. This generation is more racially and ethnically diverse. Regardless of what a relationship is defined as, there is more equality. Life is more global…the world is to be seen and experienced.

Gen Z are children born after Gen Y. I cannot begin to predict the changes that will occur when this generation comes of age and into adulthood, under the surge of this dramatically shifting global entity.

With many generational changes occurring over the last one hundred years, one piece of intelligence remains consistent, yet often underestimated. What children experience in their upbringing, (regardless of the number of, or the dynamics of the caregivers) has a profound effect on their entire life. Their stuffing will define years of health and opportunity or disease and struggle. Changing cyclical and negative social patterns, requires a huge investment in the wellness of children.

I believe children require strong bonding and mentoring by both (healthy) parents, (or a responsible caregiver), to develop healthy self-esteem, life skills, mental wellness, physical energy, and team work. There is exceptional research to back the importance of healthy bonding between parents and a child, and how this affects the future trajectory of the child's life. A child who experiences abuse, trauma or emotional disconnection in childhood, has the odds stacked against their future.

One of the books related to this subject that I highly recommend is, *The Sacred Sick: The Role of Childhood Trauma in Adult Disease* by Robin Karse-Morse and Meredith S. Wiley. It is described as "… connecting psychology, neurobiology, endocrinology, immunology, and genetics to demonstrate how chronic fear in infancy and early childhood — when we are most helpless — lies at the root of common diseases in adulthood."

The author highlights case studies and scientific findings about how our inborn fight-or-flight system can injure us if overworked in the early stages of life. Persistent childhood stress can trigger diabetes, heart disease, obesity, depression, and addiction later on. I agree wholeheartedly.

A parent can provide a home, a bed and food, but, if they do not connect with the child through intentional, healthy and positive interaction, this lack of connection has the same long-term damaging effects as those children who experience trauma and chronic fear. It's sad to say, but these kids are being set up for a future full of problems.

Care for those *Baby Piñatas*! They need and deserve love, communication, learning, participation, a wholesome environment and so much more to be healthy: physically, emotionally, mentally and spiritually.

Chapter Six
My Broken Chooser:
Baby-doll was Baby-dollar

Jack called me "His Baby-doll," which my Dad later referred to as "Baby-dollar." Jack was a lawyer, yet had little to show for the title. I put the majority of money down on our matrimonial home.

When I met Jack, he said that he checked the local property registry to see if I *owned the home* that I lived in, which was located in a nice subdivision in town. He was pleased to discover that the deed was in my name, only.

Jack said that he did not want another one, like the last one. He was referring to the deceased mother of his three children, who took her own life. He accused her of costing him money, but I'd soon discover, Jack was likely the source of any money issues they had. He was an animal in a cheap knock-off suit. Everything about him was phony. Early on, I should have stopped listening to his complaints and walked away.

I later discovered that I had a *Broken Chooser*. If you wonder what I mean by that term, read on and I'll explain.

We humans aren't born with an operator's manual. Through my time with Jack, I learned a very difficult lesson that allowed me to see my flaws and grow from this experience. This is where I discovered the value in seeing life-altering events as foundations of growth. My Broken Chooser taught me how to see my Piñata Stuffing through honest eyes.

Dear Piñata,

When we blame people or circumstances for our troubles, we are not focusing our energy on where it needs to be, on us. When our Piñatas are picking dysfunctional lifestyles, not living our purpose, or forgoing our goals, we need to ask, what is holding me back?

When we are strong internally meaning a well-balanced Piñata, we make healthy and loving choices in our lives.

The Broken-Chooser Piñata – Reflecting Upon and Evolving from Flawed Stuffing

In my post-psychosis, Frank, a friend of the family, said "Char, you have a broken chooser."

I asked Frank to repeat that statement, puzzled by a phrase I'd never heard of. "A what?"

Frank said, "A broken chooser."

He then added, "Your chooser is broken, but it can be fixed."

My mate chooser was filled with unhealthy concepts about relationships and low self-esteem stuffing that I had gathered throughout childhood and adolescence. I was addicted to fixing others at the expense of my own wellness.

Piñata Ah Ha Moment

Is your chooser broken? Do you need to repair a few bugs or do you need reprogramming? Remember, your chooser extracts data from your past. To be a healthy, happy Piñata, you need to digest new data that will help you, not keep you stuck.

The Un-stuffing of My Piñata

After the fallout in 2012, I had to fight to get my life and sanity back, so I could start over again.

During the course of several months, I met with a psychologist, a psychiatrist and my family doctor. All pegged this out of character episode as a psychogenic stress reaction caused by abuse from my then mate and his children.

I met several times with a psychologist named Jacqueline. After many aptitude and sanity tests, I was thankfully rated as sane, intelligent, and well-spoken.

Tears rolled down my face as I said to her, "How could I have been so stupid. I must be the biggest fool in the world for being taken by a man who used me for my kindness, money, and sex."

Jacqueline said that many very smart men and women have been taken by others who con them, sweet talk them, promise them the sky and they are givers who are sucked down the drain by the takers.

I felt somewhat relieved to hear that I was not a complete fool, yet, rather naïve. Jacqueline spoke to me about my childhood. She was trying to find the root cause of how I became a fixer and a giver and had no value for my own well-being.

Looking back, I shake my head and think, *What the hell was I thinking?* I picture Dr. Phil looking me straight in the eye while sitting on his stage. Under the microscope of the lights, camera and his audience, he says, "How's that working for you?"

"Not good, *Dr. Phil.* Not good"

When I made the decision to marry Jack, I certainly had a brain. However, I was also pre-programmed by the stuffing in my subconscious mind. That stuffing taught me to rescue, fix and work like an exploited care giver in order to be loved.

Think about your relationships and some of your choices in the past. *Were they made from a healthy state? How have you evolved from your past? Are there things you can change today that will produce better outcomes in your life?*

Jack's last wife committed suicide. Initially, I felt sorry for him and his children. I was unaware and oblivious to the fact that I was about to become Jack's next victim.

When I met him, I had just ended a second marriage and was looking for Mr. Right. Thinking he was intelligent (pull out all your best lawyer jokes), I figured I hit the jackpot. I hit the jackpot all right! I nearly lost everything I'd worked for my entire life for. But not only were material things in jeopardy, I nearly lost my most valued possession. Charlene.

My Piñata was hit really hard.

The Piñata Theory™ Greeting Card Collection

You will find a link to my Piñata Greeting Card Collection based on The Piñata Theory™ at the end of the book. These cards are meant to encourage and inspire others during life's memorable or challenging moments. One of the cards displays a colorful and charming Piñata rubbing his head. A little bit of his stuffing is coming out. The caption reads: Heard You Got Hit Pretty Hard. Every card has a different picture with a special message.

Did you know that you and I were born to bounce back, survive and thrive? Never give up on any situation, even though it doesn't appear hopeful today. Things can and will change, when you keep focused and put effort into physical, mental, emotional and spiritual wellness. One day at a time, one step at a time.

Jack was a fixer-upper. I fed off of this type of relationship. I'd dive in and be the *Superhero Piñata* — fixing him and his life. Do you behave like a *Superhero Piñata*? Do you feel it necessary to continually rescue others?

I felt it was my duty and obligation to do so. I was a martyr. I felt so good inside when I pleased him and cleaned his house — even when it was trashed beyond belief. It was a dump.

I used a shovel to remove pails of dirt off the floor in one room, including dog feces. Smashed walls, rooms full of garbage, abandoned exercise equipment, and junk from wall to wall ran me ragged as I attempted to clean up his chaos. Looking back, it was a real-life horror picture. My focus was making it better for them. Holy Piñata, my stuffing is doing a back flip right now.

Tips for Growing Healthy Piñata Relationships (with self and others):

- Are you an over-worked Piñata? Eventually, when you burn the Paper Mache at both ends — you are going to burn. Ouch, my Piñata hurts. Balance your life so that you have alone Piñata time. Rest when you need rest. If that means hiring help or delegating choirs, do it. Your health comes first.

- Are you doing everything for another Piñata(s) and nothing for you? It's nice to give, that's not the point — when you give all your candy away — you will be empty. You won't know what knocked the stuffing out of you. It will sneak up on you like a kid with a stick. Double ouchy!

- Are your relationships healthy? Take a look at your significant Piñata relationships and honestly evaluate the positives and the negatives. Always put your best colorful foot forward, meaning, give love, kindness and fairness in all situations. When you've hit a roadblock, consider counseling. When is it time to stay or quit? This will be unraveled in what I call Piñata BS Stuffing later in this book.

- Share Responsibilities. Piñatas in relationships need to share all responsibilities, inside and outside the house. Baby Piñata's need two loving parents or parent figures. If you are dating, treat each other with respect, love, kindness and truthfulness. Dating is a testing ground so to speak. It's a way to find a Piñata that compliments your values and life, to see if a long-term relationship is worth pursuing.

- I know awesome Mommy and Daddy Piñata's who put their spouse and children first. These are the healthiest relationships because these Piñata's are connected, spending quality time together, learning, sharing, growing, encouraging and loving together. Statistics show that the future life trajectory of children is better when strong parental connections are made at an early age. Quality Piñata Time is priceless.

For months, I worked on climbing out of a very dark hole. I was a broken Piñata. It didn't help when my Mother said I had *sucker* written across my forehead. That upset me when she said that, as I thought — *who was my teacher?*

In the past, Mom did a lot of giving, to a lot of people, and was the rescuer to my father and any stray cat that needed a place to live. Dad was a seasoned drinker and our house was a party place for some of the local drunks who never seemed to have enough drink in them. It was sickening.

I remember being five or six and walking through the room where all the drunks were pouring booze, well on their way to extreme intoxication. One particular time, my dad said, "She's ugly," referring to me. All of the drunken men laughed. I frowned and they laughed more.

Subsequently, my parents would make fun of me when guests were at the house by saying, "look mean" to which I'd frown, resulting in laughter. That stuffing was confusing and painful. I absorbed it, without choice.

I was the youngest of six children, closer to age to three brothers. Two picked on me regularly and one shamed me in front of his friends. I was overweight. I downloaded truck-loads of poor self-worth and self-esteem stuffing.

In high school and in my early teens, I was anorexic, thinking I needed to be thin to be loved. I was 115 pounds, 5'6" and a size three was loose. While a teenager I contemplated an overdose to escape. Luckily, a friend helped me through my roller coaster of emotions.

I drank and used drugs. I had boyfriends, friends and lived the party life. At the age of sixteen, I rolled the family car. I was highly intoxicated. Luckily no one was injured. My brother rolled a car intoxicated within a week of my collision. He survived uninjured. It was quite the telling tale of the state of our home, having two wrecks parked in my parent's yard.

A *Piñata-Cat* gets only so many times to land on their feet. Then they aren't lucky anymore.

My Mother was working around the clock and would go to the local watering hole (bar) to get my Father to come home to watch us as she had to go to work the night shift. That was after she did all the cleaning, caring for the kids, washing clothes and running herself ragged. She looked worn all the time. It seemed she needed to do more, to feel like she was more.

It was her way of getting approval. The approval she never got from her mother who was bitter when my mom married pregnant to the local party boy. I did the same as my mother. I worked myself ragged and overcompensated for someone else's lack of responsibility.

My mother tolerated this life for several years and claimed, "What was I to do with six children?" Dad was handsome, hard-working and a good provider, however, I don't remember having any discussions with him (one on one) on a regular basis, or throwing a ball, or even him reading to me or tucking me into bed.

I can remember lying under the bed sheets while all the party noise filled the house. Dad worked in an auto factory, did farm work and relaxed by partying with my uncle and other drunks who to this day are either deceased or chronically brain dead from so much booze.

Mom and Dad did the best they could with what they knew, believed, needed, struggled with, desired — all components of their life experiences. They, after all, were very young and had so much more to learn in life. I have made plenty of mistakes myself. The best we can do today is to learn from our mistakes and to forgive. As we'll see next, sometimes we learn best from watching and listening to others.

Chapter Seven
Time-Related Stuffing

My parents are elderly now and married 65 years, a great feat in this day. They say that old people are wise. I agree. They lived and learned, many times, the hard way. They have seen a lot.

Sit with any elderly person and you will soon appreciate the gift of life. They reminisce about or admit failure, successes, changes, tragedies, blessings, losses, lessons and victories. The stuffing that a Piñata collects over 70, 80, or 90 years is fascinating. These elderly charms speak from experience and know it best. After decades, they've discovered that the status quo (fitting in, money, titles, and material stuff) was not as important as the make-up of a person. The most important thing in life was growing in love, faith, character and service.

Along the way, these people had, or chose to, kick some of their unhealthy stuffing to the curb, proclaiming — *This is wrong or this is not who I am.* They analyzed life's deepest questions — *Why am I here? What do I truly need, want or believe?*

My parents are wonderful people; they did the best they could at such a young age, with the life they faced. My parents instilled in us to love, to support each other and to work hard to get ahead in life. My brothers and sisters have all done well and thankfully the oldest three have remained in long-term healthy relationships.

Yet, my two youngest brothers and I seemed to pay the biggest price for growing up in an unhealthy (alcoholic) environment. Dysfunction and substance abuse was hurled upon us, with no place to run, except maybe to the barn.

I suspect that deeper and more traumatic experiences occurred. Some of this secret stuffing has been well secured and locked. The key was tossed away long ago. I believe however, that secrets eventually surface, given time.

Human-Made-Stuffing Changes

My parents had stuffing loaded into them beginning in the 1930's. Their parents had stuffing from the 1800's. Take a moment to wrap your Piñata brain around that. Consider all of the dramatic changes in people, technology and the planet in 100 years.

Today, stuffing is coming from all directions and from new sources never seen, heard of, or experienced by past generations.

Current and past generations have *time-related stuffing*: belief systems, tools, peace or war, famine, disease, gluttony, health discoveries, and so forth.

What will be different 50 to 100 years from today? There will be life styles, things and discoveries we can't even fathom currently.

Will wars continue? Will peace be the new standard for the planet — where all nations work for one and all?

Perfect Stuffing from God

In spite of all these changeable and unpredictable components of human-made stuffing, one thing remains consistent, pure, perfect, limitless and unchangeable: *God and Our Spirit.*

God is the same today as He was a million years ago, as He will be in a million years from now and into eternity.

Spirit is the part of us that is *God-Loaded-Stuffing.* Though it's not really *stuffing.* However, to remain consistent with theme of this book, let us envision it as coming from God and placed in you.

Spirit is the essence of life. It patiently waits for the mind, body and human-made stuffing to relinquish control. I will talk more about your spirit (yes, you have one) and *God's Amazing Stuffing* later in this book.

Chapter Eight
Your Piñata Shell (The Body) and Mind

Stuffing is something you put into something else. You can stuff your suitcase full of clothes, you can stuff your face with food, you can stuff your body into tight fitting clothes, stuff a stocking at Christmas time or someone may tell you to *stuff it*.

Stuff can fill your home, your mind and warehouses. Stuffing can take on many meanings, depending on the context of the situation.

Your data bank (subconscious mind) is stuffed full of memories, experiences, sounds, words, pictures, feelings, education, religion and so much more.

Our *Piñata-Shell* is made of bones, skin, muscles, cells, hair, a liver, a heart, lungs, teeth and a brain. All physical stuff that is touch-able (well most of it).

These descriptive words create a picture about your physical Piñata and your mind, which is the running transcript of your life.

We consume food into the physical body, which is necessary for health and maintaining life. We also consume things that are stored inside our mind. Pictures, words, smells, sounds and worldly experiences are translated from the exterior physical form, into thoughts and memories, captured and stored within the mind.

The Dueling Duo: The Subconscious and Conscious Mind

There are two minds that co-exist within your brain — the subconscious and conscious component.

You don't need a brain and head the size of Godzilla's to hold all of the information contained within these minds. It is remarkable however, that our brain can store an incredible amount of data — everything we have accumulated since birth.

The subconscious is a data bank of what you have experienced/learned in the past and the conscious mind is your mind in the moment.

Conscious means awareness. You are awake, alive and aware, stepping through daily life. Your conscious mind is receiving the words in this book, transmitted through your eyes to your brain, translated into a message, to which we take what we perceive to be the meaning or truth. Your conscious mind makes choices and analyzes information to make decisions, taking into consideration that your deeper subconscious mind is always running in the background, ready to provide input based on past experience.

When you were learning to drive a car, your conscious mind was carefully thinking about each and every detail, step by step. *Where's the gas pedal? There's a stop sign ahead. I need to prepare to stop. How hard do I push the brake?*

Because you were learning something new, you had to focus your full attention, mainly because you did not want to get into an accident. You also wanted a driver's license. Perhaps you were nervous, scared or apprehensive while learning to drive a car. Those feelings came from your subconscious data bank, because you experienced nervousness, apprehension and fear in the past.

Be aware that the subconscious data bank triggers feelings in the moment (now) based on past experiences.

Your subconscious mind feeds your conscious decisions, many

times causing repetitious behavior. The subconscious mind is within us, like a hard drive in a computer. It drives us, unconsciously and automatically. This is positive and necessary in many ways. For example, your body is automatically functioning right now thanks to your subconscious motor. Imagine if we had to consciously say to our hearts *beat, beat, beat.* We need our subconscious minds to keep our internal body systems functioning.

Your subconscious mind aids in protecting you, by remembering, for example, a hot burner will burn my hand. When you decide to drive to the store to pick up groceries, the automatic driving of your vehicle comes from past learning experiences that are etched in your subconscious mind. Of course, you are conscious, still paying attention, but the skill is not new.

The minds collaborate, yet the pull or influence of the subconscious mind is thousands of times more powerful than the conscious mind. This is why I referred to these as dueling minds. The subconscious mind aids you by storing useful information, yet it can also limit your potential due to the source, truth or accuracy of the stuffing. It is advisable to know how the latter mind influences you so that you can consciously step in and over-ride the old stuffing with better stuffing.

Now that you know more about how your mind functions, I'd like to share a life-altering tip – don't get all tangled up in your old stuffing. The following chapter explains the importance of letting go of the things we cannot change, and beginning anew each day, releasing our struggles to God.

You and Your Stuffing

So many things happened to your Piñata since birth. There are no two Piñatas who are exactly the same. Are you also aware that every Piñata has unique fingerprints? No two prints in the world match. I often ponder, with millions of people in the world, how can every fingerprint image contained within such a small area be completely different? Similarly, unique identifiers within DNA — your blood print

— is totally unique to just you.

I fingerprint people regularly, working for the police. Some share their story about how they came to be on the wrong side of the law or addicted. Life experiences had a tremendous impact on their dilemma.

Every Piñata is flawed to varying degrees due to unhealthy stuffing collected along the way. People have the conscious ability to make decisions, yet many are chained to their subconscious mind (the past) which can limit them or make them believe that they are not capable, lovable or good enough. This is a dis-ease of the mind as the person draws from an internal well that was filled more so with circumstance versus choice.

Situations from the past may prevent a person from forgiving another person. The hurt Piñata holds on to the pain like a monkey holding a banana. The banana or pain becomes their story, they feed on it. They don't want to let go of the banana. Everyone can see the banana. The banana is their ego. It becomes a symbol of, *I was right* and *he or she was wrong*. Ego loves to be right, (or believes it is justified) regardless of the cost.

I believe the biggest obstacle that we have in our life, is the result of being trapped in our own minds. Joyce Meyer wrote an amazing book called *Battlefield of the Mind*. Joyce is a compelling Christian author and speaker from the USA. She explains how we can become trapped, limited, depressed and fearful from turning the same old information over and over and over in our heads. It's like a hamster wheel. The little guy is running, running, running, but is not going anywhere. He is stuck. Meanwhile, the poor little guy gets a hamstring (pain) from all that running. He cannot move forward.

Joyce speaks about worry, doubt, confusion, depression, anger and feelings of condemnation, as attacks on the mind. Joyce and I are on the same page — in order to change your life, you need to change your mind. That happens, by consciously being aware of these feelings and nipping it in the bud, before they take a stronghold in your mind. Joyce teaches how to deal with thousands of thoughts that people think every day and how to focus the mind to the way God thinks.

This one is golden and more valuable than precious metal. The key to change happens when we transform from mind (mostly man-made) to spirit (God-made). When we digest and wholeheartedly accept the word of God as the authentic source of wisdom, truth and hope, our life becomes easier to navigate through. When we ask God to guide us in every decision that we make, we are seeking his leadership. When we choose to shift from unhappiness to gratefulness, life becomes precious, colorful and beautiful beyond measure.

We can choose to shift from hate to love.

We choose to shift from anger to forgiveness.

Joyce Meyer wrote in her book, *The Battlefield of the Mind,* "Our past may explain why we're suffering, but we must not use it as an excuse to stay in bondage."

When Joyce refers to our past, that's what I refer to as our stuffing — what's been downloaded into us — many times, without choice. We can choose to keep unhealthy stuffing and keep suffering (recognizing there is a problem) or say, *I've had enough, I want to get off this hamster wheel. I know there is a better, healthier way.*

We are quite the same when we are stuck or trapped in our mind, we eventually become sick — filled with anxiety, depression, anger or fear. We burn a lot of unnecessary energy as well. Joyce explains how the mind is of the flesh. Joyce encourages us to get our wisdom and encouragement from the Bible, from the Word of God. Not a bad idea, considering he made our minds and as we'll discuss in the next chapter, he planted a part of himself inside us.

Chapter Nine
God's Amazing Stuffing – the Best Stuffing Comes from Heaven

God is flawless and He has planted part of Himself in us — we are filled with *God's Amazing Stuffing*. I'm not trying to belittle God, by saying He's stuffed us. But according to His own word, He's provided us with a spirit — which is a piece of Him.

The spirit is separate from the body and mind. It's not something that can be put on a scale and weighed or compared to someone else's.

We are all born with a spirit. It is a gift from God.

Your spirit is within you. It is not included on the human anatomy chart or taught in school. The spirit can't be seen with the eye. In scientific terms, some Piñatas concur that, *if you can't see it, it doesn't exist*. Their *show-me-proof-stuffing* was downloaded into their subconscious mind long ago. It came from a human-injected limited belief system — stuffing that stated, *in order to believe in something, physical proof or evidence is needed; invisible things are not real.*

I and many Piñata's around the globe have experienced connection with the unseen. I believe in the unseen, in miracles, in angels and in divine messages.

God's Amazing Stuffing speaks to us, if we are receptive to exploring beyond skin and bones. Our *Spirit-Stuffing* is an entity and voice within us that in essence, co-exists with a human body and mind. It's like a slice of the divine and a human being, all in one.

The Spirit Stuffing is honest, pure, and flawless. It is the part of us that speaks the truth. It is our inner *God-Positioning-System* (GPS) with unlimited data.

If, for example, you are uncertain about a decision, ask God for direction and wait. Be patient and the answer will be revealed. It will come to you as a message clearly intended for your spirit — through your eyes, ears and inner voice. The message could be an event, a spoken or written word, a picture or moment that will clearly give you the answer.

These messages also tell us when there is danger or when something is not right. We experience an awareness or a gut feeling, that we cannot explain — rather, a *knowing*.

I am certain, that if you stop and think right now, you have heard this inner voice. Did you listen to it or go ahead and do your own will? Think of the times you were fortunate you listened.

The spirit is our natural, inner voice. Please listen to it.

On several occasions, I ignored the truth, in order to get what I wanted, for short term pleasure or gain. The universe tried to intervene — it was literally whacking me over the head with a stop sign and I just did what I wanted to do. The universe was screaming to me, "Stop, stop!" Yet, I relied on my own pool of data, ignoring the fact that my information was flawed. Does this sound familiar?

The spirit contains the sweetest gems within, planted by God. These gems are compassion, love, forgiveness and benevolence. The spirit is fueled by your ability to use these gems for the greater good. The spirit glows when you use your gifts (delicious stuffing) and share them with others. It could be singing, writing, cooking, building, designing, sewing, sports, and so on, all of these done for the greater good.

When you are living in spirit, you are living your life purpose on a daily basis. If you were designed to sing, then get out there and sing! Share all of your Piñata's delicious candy and gifts with others. Do you have a burning desire to learn an art? Travel? Sign up!

Truth and love are the driving forces and foundation of the spirit.

When a person operates in opposition of truth and/or love or being out of spiritual alignment; this person will suffer pain and will inevitably inflict pain upon another. There is no dodging this universal law.

What we put out into the universe, returns to us like a drone on a mission. It will find us and balance the universal energy and necessary lesson. Like karma, there is no escaping it. It will remind us of our flaws until we get it right by making better choices or learning new behaviors. When we base every decision on truth and love, with benevolence for others, we will experience reward, joy and better relationships.

The *Spirit Stuffing* is also our wireless connection to *The Grand Piñata*, of all Piñatas — God. This is something to be grateful for and celebrate every day.

What a joy to know that God is connected to us, without the need of an internet connection, or a phone. He's always connected. What a reassurance it is to know that God has His hand on your life and is guiding you toward a life of joy. He's your Father Piñata after all. This is super cool, beyond measure.

Take a moment, right now. Put this book down to talk to God. Openly tell Him what it is that you need to let go of. Talk to Him and release what is on your heart. Be fearless in speaking that which you are struggling with. Thank Him for all your blessings today. Tell Him that you are committed to His guidance by not relying on your own stuffing. Finally, ask how you can be of service to Him.

Human-Made Stuffing (HMS)

Human-Made Stuffing is not at all like *Spirit Stuffing.* It often can be driven by self-serving behavior and focuses attention or worth on possessions, power, money or control. Human nature may lead us to greed, selfishness, crime, lust, lies, abuse of drugs, abuse of people, workaholism and such — all unhealthy stuffing.

These driving forces make being a human downright painful at times and out of alignment with our spirit or divine purpose. Just watch the news or surf the web and you will find many examples of people behaving like they are mainly stuffed with *HMS.*

Some *HMS* is self-centered — it looks out for #1, exploits others and is all about three Piñatas: Me, Me, and Me. I can think of many examples of *Peep-Piñatas* who have some or all of these qualities. In reality, we all have HMS which has tremendous power over our choices or behavior.

Take a moment to evaluate how much and from what source you are being motivated by — *Human-Made Stuffing* or *Spirit Stuffing.* Are you 90% *HMS* and 10% *Spirit Stuffing?* You may be 50/50?

You may say, Charlene, you said God gave us God's Amazing Stuffing, so how can it be a percentage? Because, dear Piñata, you have a mind and that mind makes choices every day, either consciously or by default — subconsciously. You came into the world with a spirit, however, along the way, you collected truck-loads of Human-*Made Stuffing*. In essence, your spirit is within you, yet, so is your HMS.

Whichever stuffing you value the most, (God's Amazing Stuffing or Human-Made Stuffing) and focus on, you will draw from. Your spirit is within you, but if it is rarely acknowledged, trusted or communicated with, then it's in hibernation so to speak. Wake that greatness up sister!

Spirit-Walkers

When you are aware of the impact of *Human-Made Stuffing* and *God's Amazing Stuffing*, you can consciously choose your decisions. Instead of automatically extracting from your subconscious mind — the place where all your human stuffing is stored, you can consciously connect with your spirit.

If you do not pay attention to the stuffing you are feeding on, your life will be limited to your human stuffing. Why limit yourself to what we humans are limited to, when you can have the *crème de la crème*?

Alternatively, those who consciously choose to connect to God's foundation of unlimited potential and knowledge, will turbo-charge their spirit and experience a more meaningful and joy-filled life.

God's Amazing Stuffing opens the door to miracles, life transformation and the *Mother Teresa's* of the world emerge. I call these special, spirit-driven Piñatas, *Spirit Walkers*. They are conductors of God.

God works through their spirit, to bring heaven to earth. These *Spirit Walkers* are highly sensitive in that they are deeply aware of global humanness and that they have a very important role. They help others reconnect with their spirit and God to experience the most enriched, fulfilling and purposeful life on earth achieved through service, love, gratitude, truth and equality for every being on the planet.

My belief is that each of us is either more human or more spiritual or a blend of both to varying ratios. I believe Mother Teresa was 99% spiritual and 1% human. She is a saint who worked with the poorest people on earth, to give them dignity and love when they were alone, suffering or dying.

When I was in my twenties, I bought a DVD about Mother Teresa. She was someone who I deeply admired. While I watched her, my eyes filled with tears and my spirit spoke to me. I knew I had a purpose here on earth and it took many years to figure out what that was. I was a typical human — I made good decisions and bad decisions and many mistakes. I believed in God, however, I fed off my own stuffing and what others told me.

This one radiates glowing purple sparkles, representing spiritual transformation. I believe that we are here on earth to transform from humanness to living in a spiritual way, with the ultimate goal of becoming a Spirit Walker. The more our life flows through spirit and from spirit, the richer our life experience will be. We will better serve the world and the more we please and serve God.

I believe that Mother Teresa became an angel when she passed from earth to Heaven and that spiritually-lead people will be given greater reward and special assignments by God when they go to heaven. They may become angels, guardians, teachers or guides.

Ask yourself — *how much do I live through spirit? How much do I rely on my own mind and other worldly influences?*

I am not suggesting that humanness is always bad or negative. We *are* human. We have a mind that chooses, and these choices may be harmful and unhealthy or amazingly awesome and beneficial.

Humans retain knowledge or experiences, such as religion,

science, math, cultural influences and such, in their stuffing. All of this knowledge can benefit mankind. And, many good people do incredible acts of love and kindness to help others.

Being *spiritual* means that knowledge, talents and unexplained discoveries are conveyed to the recipient Piñata from God. This can only occur if the Piñata is connecting with their spirit to receive this gift from God. These God given gifts benefit people, animals and the planet. Further, there is no loss or pain to anything or anyone. Spirit stuffing is pure, harmless and benevolent. How do you become more spiritually aligned? Keep reading Piñata, and be ready to devour awesome stuffing in the next chapter.

Chapter Ten
Your Piñata Radio and the Super Spirit Antenna

Imagine that you are a *Piñata Radio* with a cute little antenna — an extension of you.

Plug your *Piñata Radio* into electricity and bam, you can surf through 50 channels, each containing a sprinkle of everything you have been stuffed with since birth. Some *Piñata Radios* have more channels, some have less, based on how much stuffing they have.

Now, imagine that you are a *Piñata Radio* equipped with a *Super Spirit Antenna*. This *Super Spirit Antenna* has a direct link to God. This is what spirit is, your built-in *Super Spirit Antenna* and connection to God. That should fluff your stuffing.

With this *Super Spirit Antenna*, not only can you listen to God, you also have countless channels to universal knowledge and a built-in microphone to talk to God through. And, God hears everything on your *Piñata Radio*. He listens to every word from your mouth, every thought in your mind and every feeling deep in your heart. I am not referring to your physical heart, rather, your unseen *heart*, the core of you — your spirit. Can you name one human Piñata that can provide you with all of that? I can't.

Mentor Piñatas

Some of us are fortunate to also have wonderful mentors who guide us on earth. *Mentor Piñatas* are a gift to us from Heaven. We receive support, love and comfort from them and they equally value us. *Mentor Piñatas* are very in tune with their inner spirit and have a *Super Spirit Antenna*. They are like the *Blues Brothers* — on a mission from God.

Later in the book you will read about a *Mentor Piñata* who guided and became a sponsor for a young man who was struggling with addiction. This was life-altering for the young man. In fact, he turned his life around and he began a relationship with God. The *Mentor Piñata* was equally blessed, serving God, through caring for another Piñata. What is a *Mentor Piñata?* Who is a *Mentor Piñata?* You will discover this in chapter eighteen.

God is always sending you a broadcast signal. It's up to you to utilize your *Super Spirit Antenna*, to awaken your spirit — to be ready to tune in, listen and gain knowledge from Him. Sometimes, He stirs the spirit of earthly helpers, such as a *Mentor Piñata,* to help you navigate through a storm.

Imagine the possibilities with God in your life. You will receive and experience unlimited super high-def, *God-Cast Channels* that connect you to the Divine, the Creator, and to the Universe. This gift is *God's Soul Station* and your spirit is the entity embedded within you to make this connection possible. I guarantee you that *Bell, AT&T, Cogeco* or any other cable network do not, I repeat, do not, get this channel.

Which Piñata would you rather be? The one that is tuned into limited earthly channels, solely relying on *Human-Made Stuffing?* Or, would you love to experience a gift greater than anything you have ever received, from the best source there is — God?

Chapter Eleven
The Piñata Code™

This nugget of truth, about your ability to align with your spirit and God is *The Piñata Code™* — the realization that you are more than flesh, more than your mind and you are not confined within a limited human belief system. You are more than the sum total of what you have been told, experienced or seen from earthly sources. You are a spirit traveling in human form.

Distractions of *Human-Made Stuffing* will be thrown in your path daily to knock you off of your divine spiritual purpose. Yet, through conscious awareness, you have the ability to live in the present, versus the past — to re-route your destiny through choice and most importantly, align with spirit and God.

Take *The Piñata Code™* literally, to heart. Doing so will change your life forever. You will heal, forgive, transform, awaken and experience your life purpose and joy. Further, here's a super bonus bombshell... connecting to and receiving from God is *free*. There are no monthly fees, no entrance exams and everyone is welcome. Non-perfect people are welcome which includes all of us.

I believed in God my entire life, yet I wasn't fully connected. I eventually began to trust and listen to my inner voice — my gut instinct, which was my spirit poking me all along. Your spirit will continually remind you that it is there waiting for you to pay attention and re-connect. It's like an intermittent signal, some days it whispers, other days it screams *wake up*!

In the past, I chose not to listen to my wise inner voice, the majority of the time. I relied on my personal stuffing and all that was mixed, blended or tainted within it.

Have you ever taken a moment to read the label on the food you are buying? There may be additives, mixed in with the food, to make it taste good, smell delicious, look appetizing or have a long shelf life. You may not even be able to pronounce some of the additives or understand how they affect your body. But, you trust that it's safe, because, after all its being sold publicly. You may rely upon others evaluation, packaging, handling and stated benefits of the food.

Your inner stuffing is the same. You have a good idea of what's in there, overall, yet there are additives that were slipped in without your awareness. It was digested and downloaded. Some of it was spicy, some was salty, some was bitter and some was delicious. Parts of the stuffing had no taste, so it appeared harmless.

Your subconscious mind's stuffing has many ingredients. You do not fully comprehend the effect of these ingredients on your life because no one can unload all of the content at will. This stuffing is *powerful* in many ways. It can provide you with an overall feeling of goodness. Yet, some stuffing will hurt you or leave a bad taste, *if you allow it to.*

Here's how. You merrily go about your day and suddenly *a trigger,* which can be a song, a person, a place, a sound, a sight or in reality — it can be anything. It cracks open your subconscious mind, releasing a past memory and places it in your conscious mind.

The trigger links to a past experience. You may feel bitterness or happiness or any blend of feelings depending on how this situation affected you in the past. I will share more examples about this later in the book. The next chapter identifies ways to take charge of your life through conscious awareness, to avoid the fallout of past unhealthy, hurtful or painful stuffing.

Chapter Twelve
Transforming Your Piñata through Conscious Awareness

Let me launch this chapter with a longer, life-altering, *Sparkling Piñata Tip* to add to your stuffing, *Precious Piñata*. This stuffing is pink, representing personal power and transformation.

When you recognize that you have opened your Piñata, triggering the spillage of painful stuffing, you have to stop and recognize that this stuffing is old; it expired long ago. Use this stuffing as the launch pad to ignite your personal power.

Compare this painful stuffing to what you do with expired food. You may put some of the food into the garbage, never to see it again. You can also compost spoiled fruits and vegetables. This process results in a nutrient-rich compost that is combined with soil to plant a seed, to grow new life. In essence, building upon the remnants of something that was spoiled, to plant a seed for something that is beneficial, that serves us in a healthy way.

In some cases, we can turn a loss into a gain. We can also manifest new healthy stuffing, by using the old stuffing, not as waste, but as a foundation of growth.

You must consciously override obstructive, spoiled or expired stuffing derived from past memories, in the moment. Nip that stuffing in the bud so to speak. Clearly state: *this is the past and I am not limited to, nor do I live in the past.* Realize that this old stuffing does not benefit you and steals the joy of a glorious new day.

Like a new flower that thrives in fresh soil, be thankful for the opportunity to grow, be alive and accept the natural evolution of life.

You have control over whether you choose to relive past events with the attached emotional consequences, over and over again. Doing so is *a choice, in the mind, to focus on it* — giving whatever it was, life. There is no benefit to dwelling on the past, as it can never be changed; although at times we may wish we could. Let it go.

Pain is inevitable in life. Suffering is a choice. Choosing to suffer is something we are capable of controlling. I am not suggesting to simply forget, bury or brush off what happened. Get the necessary counseling to help you heal from loss or painful situations, particularly in cases of trauma. A doctor or counselor can help you navigate through the stages of grieving and healing, so that you can flourish again.

Go easy on yourself, *Precious Piñata*.

Use this old stuffing as a spring board of growth — learning and moving forward. Some things could have been done differently or circumstances may have been completely beyond our control. That is life, we live with Piñata's who have varying beliefs, views, knowledge — all of them have unique stuffing.

In order to move forward from the past, we must learn to override or overwrite memories stored inside the subconscious mind. This takes work, practice and conscious awareness.

It's easy enough to dwell on the past. Staying the same is natural, familiar and easy. Change takes work through establishing new patterns, behaviors and choices. Change includes learning new material, being in new settings, walking in a different direction and saying no to things and people who are unhealthy for us.

Some people remain in a state of victimhood for months and even years. Victimization can also be passed from one generation to the next. In such case, the person who was violated remains attached to ongoing defeating thoughts and patterns by reliving the event from memories stored in the subconscious mind. And, the person then repeats the behaviors that violated them, on to someone else, believing the acts are acceptable, when they are very wrong, such as sexual abuse.

In order to move forward, this Piñata needs to practice switching their internal channel or focus from the past (subconscious memories) to today (conscious awareness).

This can be accomplished by imagining that you are holding a big dial and you are turning it from one channel — *the past channel*, to *the now channel* — today. You literally move from or stop past thoughts, by switching to the current reality of today, with total focused awareness.

When you are on the *now channel*, you are in a conscious state of drawing solely from today and cannot move the channel back to the past. This is forbidden.

Some Piñatas have successfully closed a chapter of their life. They did so by doing their homework. They reviewed all of the material and considered the dynamics of the players involved. In order to pass the final exam, they had three choices (all being correct): a/acceptance, b/make peace with it or c/learn a beneficial lesson.

Piñatas can always use past experiences as a way to help other Piñatas who are going through a similar situation. Whatever has happened in the past — there is a good chance that you or someone learned a valuable life lesson, became stronger, changed direction or helped another because of these experiences.

Choose to move forward, rather than being bound by the chains of the past. Today is the only time you have, so embrace it.

Your choice to focus on today will be favorable and delicious. It will be like consuming vanilla stuffing covered in rich, creamy chocolate. Now that your Piñata is salivating, sprinkle beautiful white sparkles of love and truth on top, a gift from your spirit. Your Super Spirit Antenna will turn on and you and God will have a conversation. If you still need help in forgiving and moving forward from the past ask Him for help. Keep your eyes focused on truth and love. These tools will set you free.

Honesty is always the best route to success as you will discover through Alex's example in the next chapter.

Chapter Thirteen
Self-Awareness –
The Ability to Be Honest

A very handsome young man, named Alex has a hard time dealing with rejection. When a girlfriend breaks up (he's had a few) with him because of his excessive consumption of alcohol, Alex becomes obsessed, upset and angry.

Alex can't see the issue and focuses on all the nice things he did for her and how ungrateful she is. Alex also calls her nasty names. Ouch, my Piñata is cringing.

He is partially accurate in his summation of the relationship, in that, he did many nice things for his female Piñatas. He brought each of them out for dinner, to the show and bought front row tickets for them, to hear famous bands.

Alex needs to admit to the full truth and humility in the demise of the relationship. In spite of all the nice things he did, his alcohol and drug abuse were not acceptable and overbearing to all of these women.

Previous feelings and experiences about breakups emerged from Alex's subconscious mind. In the past, he had a very bad experience with rejection, resulting in pain. He had coped with rejection by getting drunk, getting angry, calling and texting the girl until the police became involved.

The core issue that Alex needs to resolve is his feelings about rejection and where these came from. This will take work on his part through self-discovery and counseling and attending recovery/addiction programs, which he eventually committed to.

This was a difficult process for Alex. Changing old ways takes work and self-awareness. It takes time to examine our past stuffing and the influence that it has on our current life. However, do not accept past experiences as a life sentence of pain. Work at recovery, healing, understanding and building a new solid foundation.

The most valuable suggestion I can give, when overcoming behaviors that hurt you or encourage others who are hurt, is to remember these great words — one day at a time. Take baby Piñata steps. Lasting change takes time. If you fall on your colorful tail, get up, brush your Piñata off and lift up your beautiful chin. After all, you are a child of (*The Grand Piñata*) *God.* Walk in your inherent greatness — through spirit, in truth and love.

Alex's Transformation

Here is an example of shifting from automatic (subconscious) behavior to conscious choice. Months go by and Alex gets dumped (again) by his latest girlfriend for the same reason — his drinking.

Alex now has a conscious decision to make. His feelings well up (fueled by his subconscious stuffing), and instead of being angry or hurt Alex says to himself, *I won't do what I did in the past, because that caused pain for myself and others. I will call my good friend John and meet with him for a coffee (instead of drinking) and I will attend an AA meeting to continue to stay sober.*

Boom! This is where the magic begins.

Alex is consciously aware of the *truth* (manage his drinking and behavior) and chooses to apply new coping mechanisms. Alex no longer lashes out or blames others. He looks at himself and focuses on how he can be a better person, not for others, but for himself.

Alex also connects with his spirit and God. Alex asks God for strength to make the right decisions and choices. Alex thanks God for his love and all the wonderful things that He has provided him. He admits his shortcomings.

> *God sends earthly beings to help those who truly want to change*
> *their life. Watch for them. They appear in the strangest places,*
> *sometimes, seemingly by accident or by chance.*
> *Yet, there is no accident.*
> *This was all pre-determined by God.*

When we surrender our self-centered ways and ask for help, change is possible. It's when we are closed, narrow-minded or in a state of denial, that pain continues to be part of our life.

Doing the same negative thing over and over, produces negative results.

Alex is a no longer repeating the same pattern, like a *Piñata Hamster* (aka: P-Ham) that keeps running on the same track. He chose to jump off of the dead-end wheel. His P-Ham now has a new decked out condo, with several levels, beautiful views, a fluffy bed, lots to do and delicious treats. He's doing and feeling pretty darn good.

Alex's old P-Ham was running wild on a wheel of life that was spinning out of control. That little guy was a stuck. His new P-Ham is alive, healthy and free. He evolved from boyhood to manhood.

Alex will continue to grow, by dedicating himself to a new way of living. Alex's new Piñata consciously recognizes repeat patterns and his need to do something *different*. His life and his future depend on this very important key.

His new learned responses and behaviors come from Alex's ability to *choose healthy new behaviors*. These new behaviors will produce brand new stuffing that he will extract information from when facing a choice or challenge, in the future. Healthy stuffing equals a healthy life.

Alex remained sober for months, found new sober friends and remained active in his AA program. Alex had never experienced life like this before. He is empowered, healthy and setting goals for himself. Alex knows that remaining in recovery is a daily effort. He is celebrating his wins and is devoting time to himself without adding the complexity of a relationship. Remember, we attract to us, those who are vibrating in the same energy level. When he achieves a consistent healthy state, only then should he consider companionship.

The great news is that Alex celebrated one year sober in the AA program. Today he is healthy, happy, centered and has a close relationship with God.

With the help of a strong *Mentor Piñatas*, Alex has a place to be heard, feel loved, be understood and learn, all in a safe environment. He also has accountability — reporting to his Mentor about following through with goals.

Alex's life changed dramatically. He is forever grateful to everyone who helped him, especially his *Mentor Piñatas*. Alex now picks up persons with addictions with his vehicle and brings them to AA meetings.

Alex is now serving God as a sign of his appreciation for being alive and saved. When we choose to live our way, instead of being guided

This stuffing is turquoise for recovery. When you are in recovery or working on significant life changes, it's not a good time to bring another Piñata (close relationship) into your life. Focus your energy and time on your own wellness. The relationship will only distract you from the work you need to do on yourself. When you are healthy you will attract healthy people. Wait for what you truly deserve

by God, we will not experience inner peace and joy. The next chapter reveals the beauty and richness of God's hand in our life.

Charlene Renaud - The Piñata Theory™

Chapter Fourteen
Love and Truth

When you actively communicate with spirit and God, your life takes on a whole new meaning and purpose. You experience a deep conviction or *knowing* that you have an important job to do here on earth. I'm not referring to job title, rather, how any role you are in can be a platform where you serve God and others.

A Knowing means with certainty, without question, that you have a divine calling in life. Your inner voice — the spirit, speaks to you regularly, nudging you to use your strengths and talents to aid the world.

We should all strive to serve God daily, through love, forgiveness, giving and by offering compassion to all living beings.

A life focused on truth and love will produce the best outcomes for everyone involved. Anything that deviates from truth or love eventually causes pain to someone.

Relationships based on illusion — one that hides truth or pretends to love, will eventually fail. If it doesn't fail, it is miserable or unhealthy, creating a domino effect of pain to others.

The feeling of pain can result from disappointment or loss, such as being lied to, broken relationships or from events we never anticipated. Pain can also result from being physically injured because of abuse or any unfortunate event. Every person has experienced some type of pain — mental or physical abuse, self-induced, loss and external forces to name a few.

The Foundation of Love and Truth

God is truth and love. The opposite of truth is deceit, the opposite of love is hate. Anything in opposition of love or truth is weak and begins with instability.

Think of any situation where there is hate, discord, dysfunction, or lies...any of these will lead to pain for someone. Something will fail — relationships, reputation, career or families.

God's Amazing Stuffing is here to help us navigate through life, especially when the heartaches or pain in life weigh us down. His presence provides us with peace, hope, meaning and basically, an umbilical cord that's fed by God himself.

If we have a spirit within each of us — this wonderful stuffing from God, why then is the world not perfect? Because, we all have the ability to choose, influenced largely by human stuffing. We can independently choose between right or wrong and whether to believe in a higher power. And, to add a level of complexity to the mix — every Piñata has completely different stuffing.

God has All the Answers

When you get discouraged or become frustrated about a situation, it is because you are strictly drawing upon human-made stuffing. Often, we are also influenced by someone else's view or a common belief system.

Remember, God has all of the answers, to everything. Ask God for an answer and wait. Patience is a virtue, especially in this world of instant gratification.

When faced with an important decision, I ask God for clarity. I also evaluate all situations based on these two questions: What is the truth? Is this action or decision based on love?

Once you start focusing on gratitude — appreciating all of the magnificent and miraculous things in the world, such as life itself, the moon, the stars, the trees, the animals, the mountains and so much more, our energy shifts from ego to spirit. God will provide favor upon you when you express gratitude.

When God is the center of your life, life becomes meaningful and fulfilling. He is my rock through storms. I openly praise him daily for every small and big blessing in my life.

Free-Range Piñatas

Many Piñata's resonate with *Frank Sinatra's* famous song, *My Way*.

These *Free-Range Piñatas* choose to go their own way, and in the end, the summary of their choices becomes the story of their life. They frequently devour and make decisions based on human stuffing. Instant gratification is often a main influence without consideration of consequence to themselves or others.

A decision is better made, when you are guided by your spirit, rather than the flesh — the mind and the body. Many of us have been blessed with lots of beautiful ingredients and information, which makes us pretty darn awesome, but, we are still flawed.

Along the way, we have been stuffed with unhealthy, untrue or damaging experiences that can negatively affect our personal journey. However, the spirit bases everything on love and truth. It asks, *Is this action, plan, choice or decision in the best interests of all involved?* This is benevolence — considering all involved persons. We need to ask ourselves, will this choice hurt me or hurt someone else?

Let me share an example of making a decision with a mix of human and spirit:

Bob is in an unhealthy, emotionally abusive relationship. He is at a crossroads in his relationship with Jill — even after going through counseling. Bob will also get lots of advice from other well intended Piñatas (friends and family), leading to more confusion. He may be influenced more by what others would do, and not what he wants to do.

Bob will also draw upon his own stuffing, stored in his subconscious mind. He may waver between feelings of hurt, fear, shame, isolation and uncertainty, as his relationship with Jill triggers these emotions based on this and past intimate relationships.

His conscious mind (which ultimately arrives at a conclusion), must acknowledge that what is happening with Jill, is separate from his past relationships. He may draw from past lessons, yet he needs to focus on the now.

Bob has plenty to consider, especially as he sifts through the opinions of others, on what he thinks he can or should do, ranging from breaking up to remaining with Jill.

Bob realizes that he needs to quiet his mind and step back from all the buzz firing at him from all directions. He chooses to connect with his spirit in order to seek clarity.

Bob finds a quiet space and meditates upon these questions:

- Is this relationship based on Love?
- Is there honesty in this relationship?
- Have I (we) done all that I (we) can to save the relationship?
- How will the continuation or ending of this relationship affect my children?

Bob asks God for help, admitting to his emotional confusion and feelings. He will wholeheartedly trust that God will give him guidance.

The answer will come to Bob from a messenger. This may be a person, usually not directly connected, perhaps a stranger. It could be as simple as words coming from his/her mouth. He may be standing in line with them at a coffee shop and they say something, making him feel tingles through his Piñata.

Sometimes, God will put the answer on a billboard. Literally.

This has happened to me a few times. God provided a written message. I looked up exactly at the time he wanted me to read the answer.

You may also get the answer from an unlikely source, such as listening to a radio program. For example, a talk show on the radio comes on, focusing on problems in relationships and the key issue being discussed is exactly what Bob is going through.

This happened with people very close to me. The couple had an argument about whether the male should still have past girlfriends as friends on *Facebook*. The female felt that the male should unfriend them. Why would he need to be connected to them, if he was dating her? What was the purpose of keeping them as friends?

This created an argument between them that resulted in tears, yelling and drama. The male said that the female should not control him and tell him who he could have on his *Facebook*. He said that these other women knew that he was engaged and happy. The male insisted it was nothing for her to be worried about.

It did not help that the female was intoxicated. This is never a good time to be arguing about anything, especially when feelings get blurred. Avoiding alcohol or intoxicants period, is a good start to a healthy life.

One day, I was driving these two in the car and a radio show came on — in perfect timing. The host was discussing whether a woman should be upset if her husband/boyfriend still has old girlfriends on Facebook. I turned up the volume knowing these two needed to hear this.

If only you could have been a fly on the windshield and seen the look on their faces as I turned up the sound. They listened to the discussion about the very thing they argued about the night before.

I told them that God speaks to us, reaches out to us in various ways. The exact timing of turning to that station and hearing the same story, was priceless. It was no coincidence — their guides/angels wanted them to hear this conversation.

This re-opened the discussion between the couple and they arrived at a healthy agreement that pleased both of them. And, she was sober and clear of distortion caused by introducing chemicals to the brain. Chemicals in brain = trouble.

Sparkling Piñata Tips

Do not argue when your Piñata is under the influence of a drug. Most important is making healthy choices for yourself by not using drugs. Life is amazing when we can live free of intoxication. Life itself has plenty of experiences to produce a feeling of absolute elation. Drugs distort reality and cause harm to the body, relationships, the community and the world.

Back to Bob's dilemma. What did he decide to do?

Bob was at a crossroad, so he prayed and asked God to help him. He waited, instead of making a hasty decision.

How will Bob know that his prayer request is being answered? He will not receive an email, a *Facebook* message or a picture on *Instagram*, from God.

The answer could come to Bob in various forms and he must be receptive. Bob must wholeheartedly trust that an answer will be provided. He also believes that there is a power greater than him, who has the ability to see all — the past, the present and the future. God knows all and has a foundation of benevolence, truth and love.

When we ask for guidance from above, sincerity is very important. It starts with releasing our worldly desires and opening the door to a source that has no limitations. Place in your heart, in your spirit, that this greater power will guide you in a direction that is based on truth and love. The greater power may also open your eyes to things that you need to change, if you humbly admit your faults and desire a change in your heart and mind.

Bob also needs to understand, as we do too, that it's in God's time, not ours. When we pray or speak to Him, never put a timeline on the request. "God, can you please give me an answer before Friday at 5 p.m.?" Ah, no. This is not the way to speak to God.

Trust the Higher Power and let go of the need to control, dictate, and make an order like you are going through a drive thru. It's not a wish list, either. Avoid the, *I want, I want, I want,* syndrome.

Firstly, the words that come from your mouth and the thoughts in your mind need to focus on gratitude for His guidance. Thank the Divine for everything you have. The haves are not your bank account, your fancy car, or jewels. Thank God for the roof over your head, water, health, the food on your plate, clothes on your back, your children, your life and the sunshine. The further we get away from materialism and ego, and move closer to God, truth and love, we will live in a state of awe and refreshing peace.

When we discover how much God loves us, we then can begin the journey of self-love. In the next chapter, we will explore love of self, and how it is communicated through our internal and external language and actions.

Chapter Fifteen
The Most Important Piñata to Love – YOU!

It is impossible to love someone when you don't even love yourself. You have to love you first. You need to protect yourself from emotional, spiritual or physical abuse. It is your responsibility to protect your children from watching or hearing negative behaviors from you or those in your circle.

If you are a parent, this is the most important role you will ever have in your life — putting your children first above all else and providing a healthy environment and experiences for them.

Children Piñatas download every experience, like a thirsty sponge, into their subconscious mind. Your example trains your children. Your words become their words. Years down the road, you will see you in them. Will you be proud?

Programming our Children Piñatas

Ponder this for a moment — Is mental, emotional, spiritual or physical abuse a product of love?

No, it is not.

Do cheating, lying, yelling and name calling define love?

No, it does not. These are all in opposition of love.

It is impossible to truly love, unless you love yourself first. The state of loving yourself has a direct link to the state of your spirit. Are you drawing from and living from the flesh (your mind)? Or, are you living your life drawing from your spirit and doing what is right, loving and benevolent? Sometimes, we make foolish decisions based on short term gain and of fleshly desire.

If something "feels good" in the moment, like going out and partying with your friends, you can bet, down the road, these choices are not in your long-term best interests. I'm referring to a lifestyle of partying not going out the occasional time to celebrate a special event. Partying on a consistent basis could harm relationships that you are in, may cause you to miss work, may lead to affairs, driving violations and it may lead to drug and alcohol abuse.

If you ever said, *I will never drink again*, that's your spirit telling you that a pattern of behavior is destructive. We do not need intoxicating substances, such as alcohol or illegal drugs to survive. There is nothing positive about their use. Society has accepted alcohol as being a social norm. Go to a wedding, to an event, or to someone's house, and often, alcohol is being served.

When you live through the flesh, you accept social norms as your norm. When you live through spirit, you refuse to follow the crowd and you make choices based on truth and wellness.

If your life is in turmoil, you can bet all of your sweet candy, that you have been living through the mind, or through your flesh.

Love starts within us. If you are being abused, then you must leave, as you need to *protect yourself...choosing to love and honor your spirit, mind, body and life.* If you have children, they are watching. If we accept harm in our life, they will do the same, thinking it is normal.

New relationships usually start off on a positive foot, with each person putting their best self forward. A Piñata can't hide behind their colorful camouflage forever—their true colors will eventually burst through. Fresh relationships can also test us—have we matured, or healed? Are we repeating familiar patterns? Evolving from hard-wired patterns in our subconscious mind takes much effort, as you will discover in the following chapter.

Sparkling Piñata Tips

The Piñata Theory™

To love one self, do what brings your spirit joy — anything that serves truth and love. If you are born to paint, then paint. Use your talents and gifts to live your purpose and better the world. Don't seek approval or acceptance from others to rate your worth. You will be disappointed. Love is internal (spirit centered, nurtured and connected to God) and is not a reflection of what others think of you. When you are strongly grounded and on a solid foundation, no one will shake your Piñata's beautiful spirit. The source of love is God and he is with you 24/7. People will disappoint us, God will not.

Chapter Sixteen
Old Stuffing is Sticky Business

After my wake-up call in 2012, I set out on a new journey. Somehow, the stuffing I used to make decisions from still needed major adjustment and purging. When a person goes through such a traumatic experience, you'd think they would learn their lesson.

I discovered that repetitive patterns are hard to break, especially the ones embedded deeply within the subconscious mind. Old stuffing is sticky business.

Boozy-the-Clown Piñata

In 2013, I dated a man who I will refer to as *Boozy-The-Clown Piñata*.

In the beginning, he was very charming, bringing me across the world on a romantic getaway. For the sake of anonymity, I will call him Tom.

Tom boasted to his friends, that he had met the perfect angel — me. He said I was much different than the woman he had spent nearly twenty years with. She left Tom after she tried to arrange their wedding, to which he refused to be any part of. He also referred to her as a princess, someone who spent money like it grew on trees.

I confided in Tom about the last relationship and the trauma I experienced. He sympathized, "Men are dogs. Your ex was a Pit Bull and I am a Labrador." He expressed that he was kind, gentle, loving and supportive. I thought I had finally found someone who understood me and my story.

Confiding in Tom early on in the relationship, became his weapon later in the relationship, when things went south. Like blackmail, he used this sensitive information to hurt me. I believe that people who are hurt, hurt others. It's a defense mechanism, to build a wall of deflection and protection.

Perfect time to share a Sparkling Piñata Tip

This one is Black —
as in Blackmail and Dirty Laundry.

Please, do not give up your candy (no pun intended) early in the dating game. Wait several months, at least a year get to know the other person before you spill your stuffing. Placing trust in someone after knowing them only a short amount of time has the potential to backfire. Besides, the ability to be cautious or rational is distorted when people start dating. They tend to think with their emotions and let their guard down. Don't share stuffing with someone you barely know or think you know.

I'm on a roll here, this one I will call the Sparkling Ruby Piñata Tip.

Some Piñatas play the game well and say they love you. They may shower you with gifts, romance, beautiful dinners, attention, but, wait. Their true stuffing will surface in time. No one can act like a Piñata they are not, for long. Hold on to your stuffing, like you are clenching your precious glass ruby slippers and the Wicked Piñata Witch is on your tail.

Tom was a high roller, who chummed with two locals who earned global success in restoring vintage automobiles. Tom had done well in a couple business ventures, making him well known in this small community for being a successful entrepreneur.

But Tom's irresponsibility and heavy drinking eventually depleted a large part of his windfall.

Tom spent many nights in local hotels. He was rather famous and well-liked because he would buy drinks for everyone in the bar. People called him the oldest teenager in town. Tom was 60. He spent money like he was a billionaire and partied like a rock star.

Tom said that he spent $5,000 per week in the local bars. Yes, I wrote that correctly — *per week*. This should have been my first clue that he drank too much. He seemed to be drawn to the false sense of identity, love and self-worth, through buying things for others. He believed he needed to show that he had money in order to gain attention and respect.

Tom had a magnetic personality and everyone knew him around town. It was fun being with him, as I met famous, interesting people. He had the gift of being charismatic and people generally liked him. He was a likable guy who smiled a lot. I think this was a face he wore, that hid insecurity and a lack of self-love.

At this point in my life, I was unfulfilled with my career at the police service. Tom ensured me that he would take care of me, that I'd *never have to work a day in my life*. I was not attracted to being taken care of.

I shared with Tom that I was a blossoming professional speaker and that helping others was my passion. He said, "Go ahead and save the world, but do it without me!"

This should have been my next clue — Tom was controlling. Tom wanted a *Blonde Piñata* at his side, to follow him around and make him look good. He had no interest in my life passions.

Tom drank a lot. I became very annoyed with his excessive drinking. I drank a lot when I was with him and felt uncomfortable about this. This was the life I wanted to leave for good.

Tom tried to run my life. If I wasn't by his side, such as tending to projects at my house, he'd accuse me of having an affair with hired tradesman doing work there. Insanity.

I recall sitting in his sports car, after leaving his rented warehouse condo. We were a few blocks away and he looked at me and said, "Where's your lipstick?" I said, "I don't know, I didn't *need* to put it on." He turned the car around and went back to his place because he wanted me to wear lipstick. I was an object to him.

In a matter of a few months, I broke up with Tom a few times, yet, he'd woo me back.

My subconscious stuffing was back at work. Similar to the relationship with Jack, there was lots of drama and breakups (by me). Yet, I'd get reeled back in. Repeat, play, rewind. I believe my ego drove the need for men coming to me and begging me to come back. I was needed, I was important. Yet, my spirit of truth was screaming, "Run!"

The relationships were not healthy, not fulfilling or based on love and truth.

Self-love was still not part of my vocabulary or on my radar.

Manny – My Psychologist from Montreal

I started to repeat the same relationship patterns, regardless of the pain it caused me. My old stuffing was sticking and I needed to unravel it. I knew it was time to invest in further professional help. I arranged to get counseling with 'Manny' through our workplace employee assistance program.

Manny was a psychologist. I needed professional help to dig deep into my psyche and discover why I picked the men I did — dysfunctional, psychological projects. I desperately wanted to end this cycle. I needed to be in love with me, instead of accepting any sort of treatment to feel validated.

My concept of relationships was derived from my child hood stuffing and it was flawed. I had self-esteem issues stemming from past experiences.

Manny said, "I don't know how you got me, but I'm going to fix you!"

I asked for a psychologist, rather than a regular therapist, as my problem was long standing and deeply rooted. Manny worked with me for months and my life turned around.

I did my homework, as I was devoted to changing my life. Manny said that I was a stellar student. I read every book that he told me to read. When he told me not to call or text or contact someone, I listened.

Manny would call me Mother Teresa, sarcastically poking that I was trying to save *everyone*. He said that I'd pick up every lost puppy that crossed my path.

He called me a door mat. This hurt my Piñata's feelings. But he was right.

Manny barked at me, "If you walked into a room with 100 men, you'd pick the biggest loser (he pounded points like nails into my brain), the guy with the most problems and you would try to fix him!"

Manny called me an *addict*.

I was insulted. "I am not an addict!" I hurled right back at him.

Manny said that I was addicted to drama, dysfunction and rescuing. Gulp.

Manny cracked open my Piñata. He got the shovel out and mined deep into my subconscious mind. The stuffing he extracted, helped me understand why I did what I did.

Manny said that I was stuck emotionally at the age of a teenager, as I never healed from past experiences. I was a stuck Piñata, buried neck deep, and sinking, in my own painful stuffing.

Growing up in an alcoholic home, I often experienced fear, dysfunction, drama, insecurity and uncertainty. Being the youngest of six children, with some of my older siblings often hurting me mentally and physically, I desperately wanted to be loved at any price.

I can remember a couple siblings packing luggage with my clothes and telling me I was adopted. They insisted that I was not like them, I didn't belong and they were sending me back to where I came from. I was about five and screamed as they pulled me down the hallway, to prepare me for the people who were coming to get me. Their mean games terrified me and buried horrible insecurity inside of me at a very formative age. My parents were out that night.

Monkey Piñata See, Monkey Piñata Do.

My Mom always played the role of the savior and a martyr. She worked around the clock, taking care of the house, the kids, helping on the farm and holding down a job.

Dad's alcoholism lasted many years, long enough for me to take words, images and feelings and store them in my subconscious mind.

{ Dad, made a conscious choice long ago to change his destructive ways (he had no choice, otherwise he would have been dead) and it has blessed all of us, especially him.}

Manny said I didn't have any self-worth and I was *dead inside*. I was.

Does any of this resonate with you? How do you feel when you read these words, *dead inside*? Do you feel like something is off, missing or just isn't right? Have you tried to escape pains of the past, only to hit one wall after another? Have you drunk yourself into oblivion or thrown yourself into bed with someone just to feel good? Only the next day, to regret your choice and feel like complete shit?

My stuffing *always* made me feel this way — dead inside, unfulfilled and existing.

In order to be loved, I felt that I had to work like a robot (to the point of exhaustion) and fix my mate's problems, rarely focusing on my own authentic needs. It was all about *him. Monkey Piñata See, Monkey Piñata Do.*

By golly, this was my womanly duty, to stand by my man and put *him* on a pedestal. (For some guys reading this book, you may be thinking it's time to park your *Superman* cape).

I will shed blood and sweat, to ensure that this ship doesn't sink — this illusion, this façade. I will balance everything to keep the image of my life — seemingly perfect, to others. What a &#%!@?* lie.

{"Tell Me Who Are You, You, You. Who Are You?" {The Who) Who are you?

What is it that you have been lying about, avoiding, all the while, wearing your mask?}

What was bitterly and regrettably hard to swallow, was even though I worked with Manny for months and had broken up with Tom, I picked up the phone.

I called Tom, because I was *lonely*.

Addiction. Lack of self-love.

I did a nose dive into my old stuffing. My stuffing was so full of neediness, that I called someone who I already decided was not a healthy choice in my life.

I admitted to Manny what I had done.

Like an addict, I needed another drink, another fix, another challenge. My drug was drama, dysfunction and fixing, all detrimental to my life. Old stuffing is sticky business.

Manny was not a happy Piñata. His voice, in frustration and in a deliberate raised tone, charred, "I leave you alone for two weeks and what do you do? You call the biggest loser in all of Ontario!"

I laughed at his funny, and to the point analogy, but felt defeated at the same time, hearing the painful truth. I had slipped again. If you can relate to what I just shared, be encouraged. You will slip up when you are making changes. Please do not give up. Slipping up happens, until your new normal is stronger than the influence of your past stuffing. Keep loading that new stuffing, the breakthrough will come. You will break those old Piñata ways and you will be *Rocking Your New Piñata*.

This is the point that I am hoping to make. If your child hood stuffing included drama, dysfunction, violence, absence of a parent (including a parent that was physically present, but was not actively involved in your life), drug abuse, poverty, crime - this all affects you, until you consciously decide that you are not living with the stuffing you were given. You discover that you have had enough pain, heartache and missed opportunities, that you want a better life. Your spirit also speaks to you, always nudging you to the light, to a new way of life, which is healthy and fulfilled.

In order to maximize the potential of your personal stuffing, you need to acknowledge what's inside and how to manage it. Keep reading, you are one step closer to stepping into your greatness.

Chapter Seventeen
Piñata Conscious Over-Ride

Everyone has good, healthy, beneficial stuffing — some more than others. We also have skeletons and toxins in our stuffing. No person is without pain, disappointment or loss.

In order to move beyond our past setbacks, we need to understand the dynamics and makeup of our stuffing.

When you burst open your Piñata to see what's inside, it's important to do so through a loving, forgiving and compassionate eye as you look inward. Things can get pretty messy, tangled and complicated when we place our stuffing under inspection.

Do you think angry, resentful, critical, or judgmental responses serve God? Even when we turn those emotions on ourselves? Do they bring us closer to spirit? The harshness of these words, adds further weight with no reward.

If you have knotty stuffing, I'd suggest the assistance and guidance of a *Stuffing Expert* to help you gently unravel it.

I'd recommend a pastor, a counselor or psychologist. We often think we can move through and manage things on our own, however, having a new perspective or fresh set of eyes enables us to see the whole picture instead of little bits and pieces.

Some stuffing is buried so deep, you have no clue that it exists and worse, how it's managing to mess up your life. If you have gone through anything traumatic, or experienced a complete disconnect from a parent in early life, then it's critical to be relieved (released) from negative stuffing!

You will find that un-stuffing is very helpful. It may hurt coming out, but when you understand its nature you can consciously override its power and effect on your life. Once you are unstuffed, you may cry, have regrets, feel shame and all sorts of feelings. It's all part of the healing process. Face the beast. Feel it, release it and move forward.

Remember, we are human and we are flawed by nature.

Do not pull bad stuffing around like pulling luggage around the airport, or worse — pull it around every day for the rest of your life. Some people have enough negative stuffing to fill a *U-Haul* truck!

Once your stuffing has been harvested, hang it out to dry, to wither. It will shrink and no longer have power over you. It loses its sting or potency. Please, dear Piñata, trust me on this one.

Sparkling Piñata Tips

The Piñata Theory™

Friends and family can help us navigate through tough times. It's nice to have people who care, who lend an ear or wisdom. However, be careful that you are not drawing from the same old well. We may have sources that are negative, unproductive or may even have limited thinking based on their own stuffing.

Be broad and open-minded when gaining perspective about or downloading new stuffing.

If you feel like you are spinning your wheels — contact a counselor to talk about things. It's very rejuvenating, provides clarity and you can keep your candy confidential. A professional will not share information with others. I shared with you that someone who I trusted hurt me later, with the stuffing I shared. With a professional, you can eventually unload all of your stuffing, beginning by releasing bits and pieces. Seek out options in your community. Check with local hospitals, mental health programs, EAP through employers…keep looking. Some have a fee, others are free. Written or audio resources of self-help books, podcasts or internet resources are endless.

Read, listen, learn, download, apply and grow.
What you feed your mind, you become.

The Power of the Conscious Mind

Your conscious mind is also your ally, as you can choose to make healthy choices, once you have been educated about this available over-ride. Sometimes it takes a few bumps and bruises to your Piñata to discover that a new way is needed. This is necessary to personal growth — learning through one bite at a time, one day at a time.

Consciousness means awareness — the state of being awake. Being conscious doesn't necessarily mean that you are fully aware.

Envision that you are sitting with your mate and they are talking to you, yet your mind is completely somewhere else. Your Piñata shell is physically present, yet your mind is thinking about other things, per-haps, what happened at work that day. While placing your thoughts on something else, you miss the full experience of being entirely pres-ent. Not to mention, that your mate will likely be annoyed, as you aren't paying attention, communicating fully or showing concern.

To be totally conscious, one must be focused on the space they are in, the surroundings around them and clear their mind of anything other than the moment.

Conscious Application of the Mind

Choices are largely influenced by the stuffing we have in our data bank.

Say for example, two Piñatas must choose between A or B. They may select the same answer, maybe not. Every Piñata draws from all of his/her knowledge and past life experience to make a choice.

Every one of us have varying levels of knowledge, education and completely unique life experiences. Viewpoints become more com-plex, beyond simple, A or B choices.

We are also somewhat limited to our stuffing, which affects our daily life, until we consume new information or expand into new real-ities and experiences.

Your Piñata may be scratching its head right now, asking, "Charlene, how can we consciously override the past or evolve past old stuffing? I've had the same fluff in my trunk for years, how do I change?"

Devour this Delicious Jelly Bean Piñata Tip:

When we learn something new and better, yet we slide into old ways based on old stuffing, then we have one foot in our fluff. The subconscious mind is at play. Conscious over-ride is a deliberate action — choosing the new way, knowing that it has a reward or benefit over the old way. It means stopping, thinking and re-routing, instead of sliding back.

Doing the same things over and over is easy because it is familiar, and an effortless pattern. Adding new stuffing takes work, because we have to seek it out, learn it and then apply it.

A *Piñata Conscious Over-Ride* means applying newly learned knowledge, responses, and behavior.

You and I are constantly learning and downloading new stuffing. Deliberately set out to constantly learn and grow: take classes, travel to new countries, partake in cultural events, step out of your *Piñata Comfort Zone*. I suggest doing something completely new and different as often as possible.

The wise Piñata chooses what to indulge in on a daily basis. You become the stuffing that you eat. Inside and out!

Piñatas Facing Major Challenges

Picture a Piñata who has barely the essentials to exist, coupled with depression, poverty and substance abuse problems. This Piñata has low self-esteem and has little or no hope. He becomes trapped in a cycle.

Now think about a Piñata who has lots of healthy good stuffing:

a job, supportive people in his/her realm, health, passion, a positive environment, and a steady supply of food and needs.

Which Piñata is more capable of making better long-term and short-term plans?

This is not a Piñata IQ test.

Some Piñata's who have been blessed or never had to overcome major obstacles in their life, can quickly point the finger at the struggling Piñata. There exists no empathy or compassion or understanding about the dynamics of past influences and how this affects a Piñata continuously under stressful life circumstances.

I see this often at work. I work as a Special Constable for a Police Service in Canada. I deal with prisoners every day — moving them to court rooms, to interview rooms to speak to their lawyers, feeding them, watching them and making sure the day goes by with everyone safe.

I have spoken to some of them about their life and how they ended up here, in custody, charged with breaking the law.

A high percentage of them have drug abuse or mental health issues. Their stuffing from child hood was usually dysfunctional, filled with abuse, drama, insecurity, fear and/or continual struggling.

These Piñatas sought out others to feel acceptance or get attention from, and got sucked down the vortex of addiction. Some fell through the wide cracks that exist for providing help: misdiagnosis or no diagnosis, lack of support, lack of proper care, not enough of or the right services to assist them.

In many ways the social system has failed people with mental health and addictions. There is stigma attached to people who suffer from these health issues.

In order to help these people, the root cause of the illness needs to be identified and treated. When did the trauma, disconnect or symptoms of altered behavior begin?

There are so many drugs available today, it is impossible to plug the tap or arrest every drug dealer.

To stop addiction or the sale of illegal drugs, enforcement is a never-ending solution to a problem that is not controllable. Enforcement puts a small dent in the drug machine that exists across the globe.

In order to end addiction or the misuse or abuse of substances, we need to focus on the user. What is the initial cause of the use of the drug? Experiment, lack of self-esteem, peer pressure, escape, trauma, disconnect, parental use or environment? There is always a point of contact and an underlying reason for the contact.

Working in prisoner management, I often wonder — *What was this person's story? How tough has his/her life been? What home environment did he/she grow up in?*

Some will say that's no excuse for breaking the law, referring to a person's childhood. It's not an excuse, however in several cases, the Piñatas early home environment filled him with stuffing that made him turn out to be and behave the way he does now.

Environment has an enormous effect on a person's life. I have worked with two to three generations of criminals, drug abusers and/or social services recipients from the same family. Is this a coincidence?

Each one of us needs to examine how past experiences affect us today. If things are not working in your favor — bad relationships, low self-esteem, substance abuse, insecurity, and so forth, you need to crack open your Piñata.

Start from square one. Ask yourself, *What's inside of me?*

Once we realize we are off track, do not get stuck on self-pity, grief or accepting this as a life curse. Choose to get help.

Asking for help is not failure or non-manly (or womanly). Your spirit will keep nudging you to transform. You may slip up a few times.

That's a normal part of the growth process.

We can overcome anything, once we start stepping forward, one day at a time, one small bite at a time. I suggest small bites, because big bites or big changes in your stuffing can be overwhelming and could set you up for failure. Set small goals and when you reach them, celebrate. Reward yourself with something that makes you feel great.

When you start stepping forward in a positive way, the universe is going to step with you, and assist you in your journey. Life will evolve, when you begin to make life changes.

Your positive energy and positive thoughts are sent out to the universe, where it is clearly received and returned in kind. Don't give up. I promise you — every step forward brings new situations, new people, new opportunities and joy. Doors open — things you never imagined unfold — things like what happen in the next chapter.

Chapter Eighteen
Mentor Piñatas

We can all learn from others who've walked there and lived that. They are experienced teachers, so they can give you excellent advice.

Alex learned from Dave, a mentor who was sober in the AA program for years. Dave took Alex under his wing and devoted his time, advice and support to Alex, to make sure that he remained steadfast in his recovery.

Find a mentor who can help you, it makes a huge difference in recovery or achieving something very important to you.

A good counselor or mentor will recommend resources for you to view or read. Fill your Piñata's sponge, knowledge is power. You may say, *I don't like to read* (a response from your subconscious about a negative event related to reading), yet read the material in spite of how you feel.

I absorbed dozens of books through my transformation from being a door mat with low self-esteem to becoming a woman with self-love.

While reading, I saw myself in many of the situations. I thought, *Gee, how could of have been so gullible?* This type of response, is the subconscious mind dragging up old worthless stuffing, labeling myself for doing what I did.

That's how subconscious stuffing works — it digs up old bones, old memories, and feelings. Remember this as you evolve. Focus on investing in your personal growth, expanding knowledge and learning better and healthier ways of living.

Don't be a *Silly Piñata* — repeating a behavior that you know is wrong.

When you are on the cusp of thinking you are about to slip back into negative patterns, get on the phone and connect with your mentor.

Your mentor is your responsibility partner, someone who you share successes and challenges with. Be honest with them, as BS only hurts you, and your mentor certainly wants to invest in someone who is committed.

Mentors have life experience in the goal you are wanting to achieve. They know the in's and out's, the BS, the pain, the work, the struggles and the absolutely amazing life that can be, once a person commits to working hard.

Mentors have also had to rise above temptation. They have the ability to share with another how they became tempted, slipped up, or what they had to do mentally to remain on course. They may share

You will feel better than you
have ever felt
in your life.

helpful tips that you may not have considered.

When a person is wanting to lose weight, food is a temptation. Perhaps someone has a goal to be fit, by going to the gym. It's easy to say, *I'm too tired to go to the gym.* Another person may be working on sobriety. He may say, *I'll only have one drink.*

It takes conscious effort to remain focused and have the ability to resist temptation.

Temptation is the root of much evil. Temptation leads to doing something that is immoral, unhealthy or illegal. We know when temptation is occurring, as we hear a little voice inside us saying *NO*, yet we continue on for selfish reasons. Instant gratification is a danger, causing us to detach from considering negative consequences.

Step back and ask yourself, *Is this in my long-term best interests? How will this decision or action affect me months or years down the road?*

When you do, as we'll see in the next chapter, you'll be ready to win the war for your healthy self.

Chapter Nineteen
The Warrior Piñata

Books and counseling are very beneficial ways to load new images, valuable insights and improved life-style recipes into your Piñata. Intentionally download life-altering, positive experiences and information into your Piñata. Does the thought of new possibilities make your Piñata want to dive into a delicious bowl of healthy new stuffing? Imagine how refreshing and rejuvenating this will be.

Picture yourself swimming in fluffy, beautiful, loving, energizing stuffing! Pretend you are playing in a bouncy tent, like a child. You are rolling in, absorbing and feeling the joy of amazing, empowering stuffing. This makes you feel secure, loved, protected, acknowledged and valuable. You are laughing head to toe and breathing deeply as you take it all in.

This is a preview of how you will feel, once you embrace new stuffing and shed some of the old, unhealthy and limiting stuffing, that you have carried for months, years, or perhaps a lifetime.

The healthier your stuffing is, the better your life will be. The more informed you are, the safer and wiser you become. Eventually, the old stuffing in your subconscious mind loses its impact and potency.

When you experience new things, you are creating a new reality. This new reality is stored (stuffed) in your subconscious mind. The benefits of healthy lifestyle choices, multiplies tenfold over time and in many ways, never imagined.

I promise you it does.

I have witnessed miraculous life changes in Piñatas who rose above major obstacles in their life. They experienced nearly unbearable pain, loss or disappointment.

Some contemplated giving up. Others thought about ending their life. Yet, they knew inside, that wasn't the way to go. Their life would be shattered, as would their network of Piñatas.

The Warrior Piñata

A Warrior Piñata is a brave Piñata, who has experienced struggle, yet displayed perseverance and courage, fighting for a worthy cause. Their common mantra is — One day at a time, one step at a time.

I applaud these Warrior Piñatas for not giving up, for embracing change, and applying healthy options to improve their life, or other's lives. They worked hard to learn a new life and earn their wings of success. It wasn't easy to do, but they remained steadfast and never quit. They did it, so can you.

One beautiful Piñata told me that he never would have imagined life could be so much fun without alcohol. He is now seeing things from a whole new perspective. This is a great example of a Piñata Aha Moment — when we feel joy through every cell of our body. We appreciate life, our body, the spirit and would never go back to unbalanced ways.

This is the way life should be, seeing and experiencing all of its beauty without distortion. It is a moment of realization, inspiration, insight, discovery or understanding.

Seek Immediate Help

If you ever feel life is unbearable, feel trapped or hopeless, have experienced a life-altering, traumatic event, loss of a job, end of a relationship, or if you internalize thoughts about harming yourself, seek immediate help.

Speak to family or friends, call a help line, call your mentor or call 911...do something. Reaching out to supportive peers or professionally trained emergency personnel, along with words of encouragement and support services, will make a huge difference.

If you are suicidal or want to harm yourself or someone else, call 911.

After attending a training workshop about suicide, I had a real eye-opener. Interviews were done on survivors of suicide attempts, specifically persons who jumped off a bridge. What do you think went through the person's mind after they jumped? They thought, I want to live!

One second can destroy a life or save a life.

Chapter Twenty
Addiction: Filling the Void Stuffing

After being raised in an environment and culture that promoted alcohol as an acceptable and normal part of life, I chose a new way.

It was easier to transition, when I started dating Stacey, who was a non-drinker. Stacey is very spiritual and has committed his life to helping people overcome addiction. I learned a new way of life, seeing life through his eyes.

Since the relationship began, I have created a new reality, by avoiding alcohol, knowing it is not my friend or necessary to my social needs or spiritual values. I unstuffed my experiences involving alcohol and truthfully acknowledged the truth.

The Mammoth Piñata in the Room

Here are the possible and real-world outcomes of alcohol consumption: dangerous or risky behaviors, sexual assault, health complications, marriage break-ups, gambling, addiction, injuries, embarrassment and even death. Other than supporting wineries, grape growers, beer crafters and raising tax dollars, there is no need for us to drink alcohol to survive.

When you are transforming and unraveling your stuffing, changes can be painful and difficult only because you are not falling into famil-iar and easy patterns. It takes work to change your stuffing.

I hear it often from people with addictions, smokers, drinkers, "It's an addiction and it's hard to stop." They are absolutely correct in that statement.

Addiction is known as a disease. I often thought, *Really? How can addiction be a disease?*

When I think about diseases, such things as cancer, diabetes, HIV and others come to mind. According to my significant other Stacey, he stated, "the disease model is based on the premise of demonstrated behavior/practice (pathology), its natural state, and its ability to progress or mutate into its fullest natural state."

Addiction as a disease means the person has a demonstrated behavior/practice.

Let's consider an alcoholic. The alcoholic has a demonstrated behavior or practice of consuming alcohol. The second part of the equation is the link to disease — the ability to progress or mutate into its fullest natural state. The alcoholic progresses from drinking socially to abusing alcohol, to the point that it is damaging his life, his relationships and anything connected to him (or her). Health and social implications continue to decline.

Similar to other chronic diseases, addiction often has cycles of relapse and remission. Untreated addiction or non-participation in recovery programs can lead to disability or an early death.

Addiction includes three consistent components – biological, psy-chological and social aspects, as I will describe further on.

{There are various degrees of addiction. What I really would like to make a point about, are weekend alcoholics. These are people who can maintain jobs, relationships, hobbies, yet have the need to get drunk every weekend. Friday, Saturday and Sunday are focused on drinking, socializing, drinking, playing, drinking, boating, drinking. If

anyone ever accused them of being an alcoholic, then they would be very defensive. The truth is, getting drunk every weekend or quite often for that matter, could be during the week, is very unhealthy and will affect the person in some negative regard. The key is whether the person recognizes this, enough to change. It is especially difficult in societies that celebrate mostly everything with the use of alcohol. A person who is spiritually solid will detach from this lifestyle, knowing that doing so is not aligned with holistic wellness.}

The Stigma of Addiction

If we think of cancer, the cells in our body have a demonstrated behavior/practice in their natural state. The cells become cancerous, when they progress or mutate, becoming damaging to the carrier.

Cancer is a disease, as is addiction, as are mental health issues. If not treated or managed, these diseases become worse, eventually untreatable or even fatal.

Why, then, are most people less compassionate about those who are *addicts* or those with mental health issues compared to other diseases?

I can only guess, these people believe that persons with addiction have a choice to stop. They do have a choice to stop, but they can't.

If it was that easy *to just stop*, why then are countless people worldwide struggling with addiction?

This person's subconscious stuffing handles stress, abuse, mental health issues, and self-esteem inadequacies with repetitious patterns and behaviors that have a stronghold on their mind. Abusing a drug or substance and getting *high* is a way to avoid reality and numb the pain of facing it, or repressed feelings, resulting in a psychological dependence.

The progression of the disease of addiction, becomes an emotional (psychological) and physical attachment, referred to as dependence. The person uses drugs and/or alcohol enough affecting the motivation and reward chemistry and circuitry of the brain (biological). If the user tries to stop using, they experience withdrawals (physical) such as pain, anxiety, sweating, vomiting, diarrhea and other symptoms, resulting in drug cravings and *dependence* just to make the pain stop. They also believe they cannot get through the day or handle life issues, without the numbing effect of the drug — resulting in a psychological grip.

The ugly part about the disease of addiction is, using a drug such as alcohol in most cases started at an early age — tweens and teens. They haven't the maturity or common sense to realize the risk they are taking, saying, *I just want to try it once.* What began as a social or innocent use of a substance (experimentation), can transform into abuse of the substance for many reasons. A common statement, such as, *I need a drink* after a stressful day, becomes a pattern, associating alcohol with stress relief.

Movies, clubs, dance halls, liquor and beer stores — all advertise, and promote these mind-altering drinks as part of life. Therefore, widely adapted social patterns, or rituals where drug use (such as alcohol) is common — precipitate and contribute to the likelihood of future misuse and abuse.

Hence, the social component of addiction is the presence of fertile ground…the environment and conditions that facilitate factors such as (but not limited to) accessibility, opportunity, co-users, a desire to fit in, ceremonies or events, and legalization.

Using drugs as a means of coping causes further regression to the user and does not solve the most important issue — what is the root of the stress, what is the user is trying to fill, avoid or forget? The drinking becomes a further problem on top of the stress. The hole gets deeper and darker. The Piñatas hope fades and the cycle begins.

We need to focus on filling the void with the right stuffing to help the addicted person cure him/herself. At least come to a place where they can filter through all the stuffing and understand their void or the root of their stressors.

There are excellent resources available in communities to help people overcome negative past experiences or stressors, accessed via: public health, doctors, counselors and programs such as *Alcoholics Anonymous, Narcotics Anonymous, and Al-Anon, Sexual Assault Survivors Networks*, to name a few. There are many programs that provide free services or reduced fees for those with little or no income.

Curing Addiction — Inclusion Versus Isolation

In order to break a pattern of behavior, one needs to learn a new behavior.

This isn't as easy as waving a magic wand. If there was a pill to cure addiction, depression, anxiety, low self-esteem and many other negative ailments, then millions of people would be free of pain and suffering.

In the interim, the diseased person must be supported with love and compassion. I believe the cure to addiction lies in connectedness, faith, community supports, compassion and love. I have witnessed total transitions in Piñata's lives with these supports.

A View from Rat Park

A study called, *Addiction: The View from Rat Park,* was undertaken by Professor Bruce K. Alexander and his colleagues at Simon Fraser University in British Columbia, Canada in 1970.

The group wanted to test the validity of earlier rat studies that concluded that a rat exposed to morphine, became addicted and could not stop taking the irresistible drug, avoiding the water option in the cage. That in turn lead to the theory that an addicted human was in the same rat race: once you're hooked, you're cooked, (these words are not literal, but you get my analogy) summarizing that all rats and people who use addictive drugs become *addicted.*

The SFU study also concluded that past experiments placed the test rats in isolation, out of their natural group/community environment. These isolated rats were then exposed to drugs and ultimately became hooked, fueling the theory that drugs are addictive.

The SFU study also concluded that previous studies only tested rats in isolation and did not test the rats in their normal environment, with exposure to drugs, as a comparator.

Think about it. If an animal or human were placed in isolation, out of their normal environment, that in itself would cause depression and changed behavior. The isolated subject would continue to feed off the drug to numb the reality of their environment.

The SFU experiment compared the drug intake of rats housed in a reasonably normal environment, twenty-four hours a day, with rats kept in isolation in the solitary confinement cages that were standard in past studies.

Rat Park

The group constructed a rat heaven of sorts for the non-isolated rats, with the things rats like: platforms for climbing, tin cans for hiding in, wood chips for strewing around, and running wheels for exercise. They included lots of rats of both sexes, and naturally the place soon was swarming with babies. The rats loved it and the study group loved it too, so they called it *Rat Park*. I call it Rat Heaven, because they lived in an optimal environment that supported food, shelter, clothing, fun and community.

{Reminds me of the time that my kids wanted white mice from the pet store. Little did we know that the two they picked were a male and a female. Before long, there was an explosion of baby mice. Mama did not call it Mice Heaven.}

The group ran several experiments comparing the morphine consumption of rats in Rat Park with rats in solitary confinement in regular laboratory cages.

Professor Alexander concluded, "In virtually every experiment, the rats in solitary confinement consumed more drug solution, by every measure we could devise."

The confined rats consumed *"a lot more"* morphine than the socialized rats. The study concluded that the social rats consumed hardly any morphine solution but the caged rats were consuming a lot, when faced with choosing between morphine and water, regardless of the sex of the rat.

{If we consider the demise of people who have been deprived of their natural environments, stripped of their culture and identity, forced into segregation or isolation, is it reasonable to understand why addiction is so prevalent in such communities?}

The hypothesis of the *Rat Park* study is that drugs do not cause addiction. The conclusion was that, addiction to opiate drugs commonly observed in lavatory rats is directly linked to their living conditions, and not to any addictive property of the drug itself.

I agree 100%.

When people are socially or economically isolated, addiction becomes the means to fill what I call the *Great Void*. They are a product of their environment and will not get better (rarely), unless they leave the environment or there is a huge improvement within their direct social influences.

When we think about older (and still existing) prison environments, isolation and segregation is the norm, which in itself does not foster rehabilitation. Newer modern prisons have a healthier and educated theory about the benefits of inclusion/community versus isolation/segregation.

My theory is healing addiction is a community effort. The better the environment for all peoples, the better the quality of their life. The residual and domino effect of health (spiritual, mental, physical, emotional) affects this generation and those to follow. We need to build strong communities, neighborhoods, foods, transportation, education, skills and holistic support systems available to all. There needs to be connection from young to old, sharing wisdom, skills and love.

The addicted person has a huge empty space they are attempting to fill. The filler becomes any form of drug that will alter their state, including damaging chemicals that devour their organs, mind and life.

The War on Drugs is Backwards Thinking

Recovery, Harm Reduction and Education Will Save Lives.

In my high school days, there was pot and alcohol, the two common drugs.

Today, there are many legal and illegal drugs in so many forms, that it is impossible to keep ahead of the curve.

Drugs are hidden beneath our noses. There are powerful, ruthless drug cartels and dealers spread through every nation on earth. I often wonder, when traveling along an expressway viewing the landscape of sprawling warehouses in a large city, *what's really in those warehouses?* When I see transport trucks rolling down the highway, with decals of the brand they are hauling, I wonder, is that really *ABC Company* or just a front to crime?

Drugs are being stored and moved in such incredible amounts that the police cannot police it all. We are catching a fraction of the dealers. And, for the ones we do, the justice system often fails us. Drug dealers are often given a slap on the hand, except, from what I have seen of fentanyl dealers. The courts, at least in my area, are coming down hard on fentanyl dealers and rightfully so. Fentanyl is a loaded gun, a game of Russian roulette - it's powerful, dangerous and deadly. It's become a pandemic of broken lives and escalating deaths across Canada and the USA.

Another consideration in enforcement and The *War on Drugs* approach, is the huge cost of policing and the judicial system. And, from what I have seen, there is a huge amount of money spent to police repeat offenders.

Of course, no one wants crime and drugs on our streets, but how much are the tax payers paying for protection and peace of mind? I see the same offenders coming through court over and over and over.

I believe our society would be a much better place if court systems imposed stern penalties on drug dealers and rehabilitation instead of incarceration for people with addictions. Most often, the small street level dealer, who is also a user, is arrested, versus the main drug supplier.

You'd have to be in *Piñata La-La land* to think that arresting our way out of drugs is going to be the solution to crime and addiction. We can't stop all the drugs flowing through our community. We can't close all the meth labs and find all the pill producers. It is impossible to stop every drug pusher.

Piñata La La Land

Remaining in a state of denial or in a dreamy belief pattern that avoids reality.

Or, applying dated and ineffective ways to address a problem.

My theory? If there are no consumers, there will be no drugs or drug dealers.

If a product is not in demand, then the price goes down and eventually the dealer is not making enough money to make his/her business profitable. The solution to addiction lies within the user/consumer. Drug dealers are in it for the money and don't care about Pete, Sarah's, John's or Larry's life and the millions of other users around the world. Dealers are not moral and often use their status to abuse people, especially young people and women.

A complete overhaul of the judicial system is needed. Money can be better spent to educate children and the community, support recovery and harm reduction programs.

What is the origin of the root cause of addiction? The next chapter addresses the long-term effects of childhood abuse, trauma and emotional disconnection, and its link to future disease.

Chapter Twenty-One
Childhood Abuse, Trauma and Emotional Disconnection - Link to Adult Disease

To cure addiction and mental health problems, it is absolutely necessary to treat the user, by cracking open their Piñata, to examine their subconscious stuffing.

The root of suffering, is an attempt to fill a void stemming from unresolved or unhealthy life experiences. The void often occurred in childhood through trauma, abuse or a state of isolation or detachment from a parent or significant influencer.

I also believe that mental health issues are deeply rooted in childhood experience and unresolved pain.

I attended an addictions conference where Dr. Gabor Mate (Canadian doctor, author and renowned speaker) was the keynote. He spoke about his work and experiences with addicts at Canada's first safe needle injection site in Vancouver, as well as the relationship between childhood experiences to future diseases, including addiction. Dr. Mate has written excellent books about addiction, stress and childhood development, including: *In The Realm of Hungry Ghosts*, *Hold On To Your Kids*, *When The Body Says No* and *Scattered Minds*.

In his book, *In The Realm of Hungry Ghosts*, Dr. Mate states, "All addiction comes from emotional loss and exists to soothe the pain resulting from that loss. Trauma and abuse, as we define them, are certainly surefire sources of loss but they're far from the only ones. The human infant and toddler is a highly vulnerable creature, and emotional stresses of all kinds in the rearing environment can create long-lasting wounds in the psyche that a person will later try to soothe or numb with addictive behavior."

He continues, "In addition to things that do happen that shouldn't happen, like abuse, there are things that (developmentally speaking) ought to happen that don't. For instance, any sustained sense of emotional disconnection with the parenting figure — which can often happen when the parent is excessively stressed or preoccupied over a period of time — has the capacity to have this sort of impact, especially if the child is constitutionally very sensitive. In a stressed society like ours, with fewer and fewer support resources for parents, this is more and more common."

Dr. Mate also said, "We shouldn't discount or minimize the pain we carry from childhood even if it didn't result in severe neglect or abuse."

That's deep and very true. I've seen it over and over interacting with people with addiction.

Dr. Mate works with severe addicts in one of Canada's worst drug infested neighborhoods — Vancouver, British Columbia. Dr. Mate is a game-changer and assisted in creating Canada's first safe needle injection site in this downtown community. Mate and his team give dignity to the homeless and persons with addictions, by providing them a place to eat, to sleep and to get clean needles to inject their drug of choice.

There were hurdles to climb, by Mate and his team to get legislation passed to allow addicts to use illegal substances at the site, without being charged with a crime. The group had to convince the Supreme Court of Canada, that safe needle injection sites, decreased the spread of disease amongst drug users, certainly a positive, but also gave these forgotten souls a place to go to, to be heard, perhaps for the first time in decades.

The project was focused on harm reduction, through stopping the spread of disease, saving lives and compassionately providing dignity to those imprisoned in addiction; those so heavily damaged (mentally, physically, emotionally, neurologically) that their natural, original pre-drug state will never be repaired.

An attendee at the conference asked Dr. Mate, "What percentage of the addicts that you have worked with were sexually assaulted in the past?" Dr. Mate replied, "All of them." There was a huge gasp in the crowd. Is this any surprise? Sexual abuse is rampant and a hidden crime on the vulnerable.

My cousin John (not real name) spent years deteriorating from addiction on the streets of Toronto and Vancouver. John was sexually abused as a child. He experienced horrific circumstances that left dark, ugly, shameful stuffing in his subconscious mind. Victims like John become entangled in an endless cycle of mind and wanting to escape from reality.

Taking drugs feels good, for a while. But then more and heavier drugs are required, because the high needs to be more intense. Reality no longer exists.

John came into this world as a beautiful spirit and human ugliness raped him, distorted him and crushed his spirit. Chronic users will do anything to get drugs: sexual acts, stealing, picking bottles and begging.

The damage of sexual abuse on a child is a life sentence — battling traumatic memories, feeling shame and finding ways to cope with the pain. The next chapter speaks specifically to what is likely the biggest hidden crime on the planet — child abuse and exploitation.

Chapter Twenty-Two
The Long-Term Effects of Sexual Abuse

Several friends and family have disclosed to me that they experienced sexual abuse as a child or in their teens.

I've sat through countless trials listening to the sickening detail by detail account of the trauma. I believe that sexual assault is the biggest hidden crime of all. The majority of the time, the offender is someone that the victim knows — usually a brother, step-father, uncle, or other family member.

The internet is used as a means to exploit, lure and damage victims and because of its global footprint, it is impossible to police every predator. Yet, dedicated officers spend hours trying to save children and adults all over the world.

I heard such an account from a Toronto police officer who worked in the child pornography section. He became so gripped by the depth of the problem, that he coordinated efforts with police agencies around the world to seek out offenders and save children from horrific environments.

I vividly recall witnessing tears streaming down his face and watching him leave the room after he began to read a letter from a little girl who he helped rescue. It is beyond the reality of most people to truly realize what police officers endure, see, hear and feel during the course of their job duties.

After speaking with persons who have been sexually violated... you discover it is the worst stuffing of all. It affected every aspect of their life since the act(s) occurred. It robbed them of their joy, childhood, innocence, healthy relationships, comprehension of normalcy, expression, freedom, and peace of mind.

It's also a difficult decision by the victim, on whether to lay charges and make a formal police report. They would then have to relive the trauma. They are terrified to go to court and face the perpetrator.

In many instances, the accused person is a relative (or someone close to the family) and the fallout affects the entire structure of the family.

It divides families: some stand up for the victim and some support the accused. Some use denial as a form of protecting the family secrets. Everyone must focus on truth and healing. The predator requires psychological assistance. He (or she) is likely repeating patterns of their past, from their own childhood experiences as a victim of sexual abuse.

The victim is also fearful of seeing the accused in court (if criminal charges are laid), triggering painful stuffing from the past. However, with approval by the judge, the victim can give remote testimony from another room. It relieves the face to face trauma, yet it doesn't negate the very detailed questioning by the lawyers. The judge will listen to the testimony, and pays particular attention to the body language of the victim and the accused.

Victims who have gone to court, sometimes feel that justice was served, in that the perpetrator was charged, investigated, and found accountable for their actions. In some cases, the perpetrator is very old, frail and believed their transgressions were well buried in the past.

Some victims never feel justice is served, even if the person is convicted. Imagine the feelings if the accused person is found not guilty or given a light sentence in the eyes of the victim?

I would never suggest that healing from sexual abuse is as simple as a choice to think of something else. This would be totally insensitive and unrealistic. I believe one can experience great liberation, by looking at someone who experienced great trauma and was able to forgive. The victim removed themselves from resentment and judgment, focusing on God's great love and forgiveness.

Such is the story of Eva Kor and her twin sister, both miraculous survivors of the Holocaust and the infamous SS (Nazi Special Police Force) doctor Josef Mengele. Despite almost being murdered Eva forgave the Nazis, which resulted in a documentary about her life, entitled *Forgiving Dr. Mengele*.

It the spring of 1944, Eva Kor along with her twin sister Miriam and her mother, arrived in a concentration camp called Auschwitz-Birkenau. When the family exited the train, a SS guard ran up to them yelling *Twins! Twins!* A few moments later, Eva and Miriam were torn away from their mother. They never saw her again.

After being selected from among the new arrivals, the sisters were brought to the now-infamous camp ran by Dr. Josef Mengele. He had a standing order for twins — segregate and use them for his medical experiments. Most of the time, he injected one of the twins with poison, a bacteria or virus and then documented the development of the disease and the onset of death.

As soon as the test patient died, he and his assistants would then immediately murder the twin sibling — usually with an injection in the heart — prior to performing simultaneous autopsies.

About 1,400 pairs of twins were victims of Mengele's barbaric experiments.

On Jan. 27, 1945, the Soviet Red Army liberated the survivors of Auschwitz-Birkenau and brought their nightmare to an end. The Kor sisters immigrated to Israel where Miriam remained.

Eva moved to the USA to build a life and family. The pain of their horrific experience remained engrained in them. In Israel, Miriam became ill and a diagnosis could not be defined, yet she had apparently received an injection from Dr. Mengele years ago. Her kidneys were failing. In spite of Eva donating a kidney, Miriam died of kidney failure in 1993.

Since then, however, Eva's story has become one of forgiveness and personal healing. She has made peace with those who exterminated her family and who tried to exterminate her.

Speigel Online, a German news media (2005), interviewed Eva at the time of the release of the film documentary in Germany about her life.

Eva stated, "I felt as though an incredibly heavy weight of suffering had been lifted. I never thought I could be so strong."

> *Eva said that because she was able to*
> *forgive her worst enemies,*
> *she was finally able to free herself*
> *from her victim status.*

She quickly added, "Forgiveness does not mean forgetting. What the victim does, will not change what happened," she said. "But, every victim has the right to heal themselves as well as they can."

Eva told the Speigel, "And the best thing about the remedy of forgiveness, is that there are no side effects. And everybody can afford it."

If you have been a victim of trauma, you have the right to heal yourself as best as you can. Admit that you can't do it alone. Connect with a professional who can meet with you, in order to purge the experience.

As Eva stated, forgiveness is not forgetting. We cannot change the past. No one avoids pain in this lifetime. Pain is inevitable. However, suffering is a choice. Choose to release your mind from the past and live in the beauty of today.

Joining support groups is also a healing opportunity. Personally, I always go to God for healing. I trust in his love, mercy and guidance to fill my heart and mind with peace. I ask to be freed of the chains that hold me back; to understand and to forgive. I know God has my back.

I don't need to make it right with those who harm me. God knows and sees all. He will bring all to justice with the dues they deserve. He also rewards those who live in service to him; those who live peacefully, lovingly and faithfully.

Do not fear God. If you have offended someone, ask for forgiveness, get professional guidance and march forward. It is amazing what happens when we forgive others or ask for forgiveness. The walls of ego fall.

How can you and I make this world better? Find out how, by reading on.

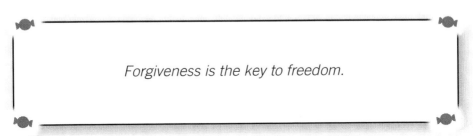

Forgiveness is the key to freedom.

Chapter Twenty-Three
Saving the Next Generation of Piñata's from Trauma and Addiction

I believe that in order to reduce instances of trauma on children and future disease, it is necessary to encourage open and healthy dialogue or educational programs focused on protecting our children from harm.

Naturally, the depth and delivery of the information is geared to the age of the child. From pre-school age onward, curriculum in schools should include healthy self-esteem, love of self and others and the importance of acceptance, tolerance and connection.

Children need to be aware of what constitutes appropriate behavior, referring to interpersonal connection, healthy relationships and the sacred value of their body and mind. Children need to recognize normal and strange behavior in adults, including family, neighbors and community.

If we simply focus on strangers as being a threat or danger, we are off the mark completely. The vast majority of sexual assault cases occur with a person that the child knows, such as a parent, step-parent, grandparent, aunt, uncle, friend of the family, babysitter, pastor or neighbor versus a complete stranger.

The most critical relationship in a child's life is that with the parent.

If a child is in a home where there is drug or physical abuse, they need to be removed and placed in a loving, safe, secure, environment. The parent(s) or adults in such situations, often faced similar life events growing up, so the abuse/addiction becomes cyclical.

> *People are mainly a product of their environment.*
> *To build strong future generations, it starts with ensuring*
> *healthy homes, schools and communities.*

If we think that what we do today has no effect on our children, we are sorely mistaken, it does! What life do we want our children to have? We must be leaders, role models, healthy parents and healthy communities. We must teach through example — give them the gifts of honesty, love, compassion, heritage, giving, gratitude, education, faith, peace, and time.

The most crucial and influential relationship that Piñatas will have in their life is with their children or with a young person in their care. When people in a parental role are mentally, physically or emotionally unavailable to a child, the child will suffer in the short and long term.

All of a child Piñatas experiences will be downloaded into their Piñatas subconscious mind and will be part of their stuffing. To grow healthy children, influential adults within their circle, must be healthy role models.

Children need love, support and quality time with their caregivers while engaging in positive activities: throwing a ball, playing games, fishing, cooking, sewing, reading and learning.

When Daddy or Mommy Piñata is drunk or drugged up, children are learning and downloading all of what they see, hear and feel into their Piñatas data bank, to extract years later. These children experience a distorted view of reality and normalcy.

In a toxic home environment, these children see and learn (and later repeat) that abusing people is tolerated, that yelling, dysfunction and drugs are normal and acceptable.

A void will exist in the child and they will look for a way to fill their void somehow, because they are not healthy. They did not receive the love and nurturing they deserved and needed to grow, learn and evolve.

Their void will be filled by someone else, usually a peer, sometimes a predator, and eventually their own addiction. I speak to many prisoners who have been involved in violence, crime and drugs and in the majority of cases, they witnessed this as a child.

An Important Yellow Caution Sparkling Piñata Tip to Remember:

Where are childhood experiences stored? In the subconscious mind. What a child experiences today will be permanent — it will always be there. It cannot be erased.

God created us equally and perfectly in every language, color, size and gender. Why then, do some people chose to treat others who are not of the same race, and belief system, in a different way?

Racism contributes to violence, segregation, fear and ignorance. The next chapter speaks of wide spread racism — how this affected innocent children, their families and communities.

Chapter Twenty-Four
Racial Stuffing

Racism is a prejudice, discrimination, or antagonism directed against someone of a different race based on the belief that one's own race is superior.

Let me give you an example of racism that occurred in Canada – Residential Schools for Native Children.

Residential schools began after the enactment of the Indian Act in 1876, which made attendance at school compulsory for First Nations, Métis and Inuit children. About 150,000 First Nations children passed through the residential school system from 1931 to 1996. At least 6,000 of them died while attending the schools.

These schools were funded by the Canadian government's Indian Affairs and Northern Development, and administered by Christian churches, predominantly the Roman Catholic Church but also the Anglican Church of Canada and the United Church of Canada.

The policy was to remove children from the influence of their families and culture, and assimilate them into the dominant white-skinned Canadian culture. The schools did significant harm to Native children who attended them by removing them from their families, depriving them of their ancestral languages, and by exposing many of them to physical and sexual abuse by staff members.

On June 11, 2008, a public apology was offered to First Nations from the Canadian Government, for the horrible injustices committed to their people, as the result of residential schools.

The Indian Residential Schools Truth and Reconciliation Commission was established after the apology to uncover the truth about the schools. The commission gathered statements from residential school survivors through public and private events across Canada.

The Indian Residential Schools Settlement Agreement (IRS-SA) a Canadian federal court-approved settlement agreement was announced by the Canadian federal government in May 2006 (implemented in September 2007), recognized the damage inflicted by the Indian residential schools (IRS), and established a $2 billion compensation package for the approximately 86,000 people who were forced to attend these schools.

The IRSSA was the largest class action settlement in Canadian history. Between 2008 - 2013, seven national events were held to commemorate the experience of students of residential schools.

The Truth and Reconciliation Commission created the National Centre for Truth and Reconciliation in 2015, and published a multi-volume report detailing the testimonies of survivors and historical documents from the time.

My partner Stacey, a First Nation Native, conducted interviews with survivors of residential schools who resided on a First Nation Reserve in Canada. These findings were submitted to the Truth & Reconciliation Commission as part of the inquiry.

The Fallout of Racial Stuffing — A Generational Plague

The residential schools eventually closed in Canada, yet a century of Native culture was destroyed. The ripple effect of the damage carries through today.

First Nation children who survived, were damaged returning to their native community. The children felt a disconnection with their culture, their families, as a result of being brainwashed that being *an Indian* was bad.

Do you recall the research I quoted by Dr. Gabor Mate and Robin Karr-Morse regarding child's disconnection with a parent and/or trauma at an early age and how this directly influenced the future health trajectory of a child?

These severely abused and damaged children, returned to their community, not knowing their true authentic Native self. They struggled emotionally, often using drugs or alcohol as a coping mechanism to deal with their inner broken child. So many are still affected today.

Residential schools, the segregation of Natives and exploitation of their land, has caused today's situation in many reserves across Canada.

The reserves have a high unemployment rate, high poverty rate, high addiction rate, high suicide rate and lack of fundamental services (schools, hospitals, services) that many non-native communities enjoy.

{*A survivor of a residential school disclosed to me in 2017 that the suicide rate is so high for youth on the reserves, mainly because of sexual abuse. He said it is widespread and that there is a wall built around the reserves to protect the truth. He tried to make significant changes to address the social issues on one reserve and he was fired, he said, "for doing too good of a job." Exposing the social elephant in the room got too close to home and too close for the predators who wanted to keep the secrets hidden.*}

Groups have sued the Canadian Federal Government and won to get equalization in native communities. It's disheartening that the Native peoples of this land are still fighting for equality, essential life services and respect.

Racism is not limited to Canada; it happens in many countries around the world and has affected millions of people for generations.

I have the great pleasure of having a beautiful, spiritual First Nations angel in my life. His name is Stacey and he is the love of my life. Stacey's parents attended residential school. He and his siblings have suffered the domino effect of parents who numbed their residential school experience with alcohol and violence.

These residential school survivors were robbed of their childhood and culture and were left permanently damaged. This in turn, became part of their children's stuffing. The children in turn, experienced the pain of their parents.

Stacey did not learn to speak his native tongue — Ojibwa from his parents, nor did he learn native culture from them. His parents were taught that speaking and being native was wrong. Stacey said that he travelled with native elders of tribes in the USA and Canada to learn the way of his ancestors.

Stacey overcame incredible odds to become a beacon of hope on the First Nations reserve where he is a drug counselor. Stacey organizes the local Pow Wow and travels to other community Pow Wow's with his native drumming group.

He also follows First Nation traditions: sweat lodge ceremonies, smudging, ceremonies for healing or of death, and celebration of transformation of the spirit. Smudging is purifying a room with the smoke of sacred herbs to help clear negative energy from a space.

Stacey abused alcohol and drugs and committed theft and drug crimes in his early life. His life-changing transformation began while he was in prison. He knew he did not belong there; his life had a purpose. One evening, Stacey dropped to his knees in his cell begging Creator (his name for God) to show him He was real. By the next morning, a large wart on Stacey's hand completely disappeared. Stacey received his affirmation. He has since been sober and helping others in his community with addiction.

Being in a relationship with Stacey did not deter a co-worker from openly mocking native people *in front of me*. I filed a harassment, bullying and racism complaint against this person. Jake (not real name) bullied me, and others, as well as degraded First Nation's people through his mimicking of them. He was found responsible for his actions and was disciplined.

Bullies like Jake, were likely bullied in the past and have low self-worth. They enjoy getting attention from others, by hurting other people. Their stuffing has a void that they attempt to fill by making others look inferior.

Racism disconnects all of us and we will never be unified if people think their race is better than another. We are all different and equal in the eyes of God. Diversity is a blessing in this world. Violence, wars, poverty and greed will continue until people unify.

Racism is fed by fanatics who feed untruthful information about people of another race, in order to create fear to justify their actions.

Piñatas who are racist have been stuffed with ill views of other peoples, from a parent, a community or a hate group. They sadly follow this belief system as though they have no independent brain at all. Stuck in their own racist stuffing, they are intolerant of those who are different, cannot be unbiased, nor make efforts to the learn about other cultures.

Remember how deeply stuffing from our past affects our decisions today? Consciously choose to educate yourself, through expanding your knowledge base from multiple sources, ultimately drawing a conclusion based on a broader view. Read about history and global populations. Do not become robotic from your programming. Be a spiritual warrior who detaches from limited human stuffing. Wise Piñatas are always learning and evolving.

Young Piñatas in Canada must be educated about the history of Residential Schools as part of their school curriculum. Some schools are taking this step, knowing the deep importance about the history of native peoples in this country. Children will be informed, inspired to celebrate multiculturalism, become compassionate about all children of God, and unite to create a beautiful world.

I am on the cusp of the baby boomer generation and I never heard anything about what happened to the Native peoples through my education. I learned about Residential Schools only a few years ago while watching CBC news. I listened in horror, about what happened in these schools and the gut wrenching testimonies from survivors.

One elderly man spoke about being tied up in a *homemade electric chair* and being zapped, "for their entertainment." Tears poured down my cheeks. I was filled with shame for being part of the white race that did this to the native people.

It is unimaginable that people, these *We are Superior Piñatas,* existed and did this to the native people. Sadly, they believed they were right.

This is a proven historical example of the real outcomes of accepting general belief systems — being intolerant of and ignorant about others.

We pulled the rug out beneath the Native (Indigenous) people, the people who shed their blood to establish this country.

The greatest Native warrior of all time, Chief Tecumseh, fought alongside the British to protect Canada from the invasion of the Americans in the Civil War.

Chief Tecumseh saved our Canadian Piñata Asses, and over time the new settlers raped, mistreated and pushed the native people into segregation, by taking their land and forcing them into smaller and smaller communities.

Stony Point First Nation (Camp Ipperwash – WWII), Canada is an example of how the Canadian Government continuously mistreated the Native peoples.

In 1942, during the Second World War, the Canadian government expropriated land belonging to the people of Stony Point Reserve (First Nation), in order to build a military camp - Camp Ipperwash. The government took the land after the residents refused to sell it.

In the years following, the band tried to get the land back, claiming it contained a burial ground destroyed when the camp was built.

Shortly after the war ended, the Department of National Defense said it was willing to return most of the land as long as it could lease back what it still needed for the military base. The offer was later withdrawn.

After twenty years, there was still no resolution. In 1993, Stony Point band members began moving back on to the land.

The military withdrew in September 1995, when another group of Stony Point natives marched onto the base.

At this time, a group of about thirty protesters erected barricades at nearby Ipperwash Provincial Park to emphasize their land claim and to protest the destruction of the burial ground. Dudley George was one of the group's leaders.

Dudley George and the Stony Point natives took over the camp in 1995. The Ontario Provincial Police moved in on the protesters to remove them from the park, which led to a standoff. Sgt. Kenneth Deane of the OPP fatally shot Dudley George in 1995, claiming Dudley was armed.

In 1997, Deane was convicted of criminal negligence causing death after a court ruled he did not have a reasonable belief George was armed. An inquest into Dudley's death started in July, 2004 and ended in August, 2006. A resulting report was made public on May 31, 2007 with findings and recommendations.

What became evident in the inquest, were the racist remarks made by OPP officers about the native people.

In 2015, twenty years after the standoff and death of Dudley, The Chippewa's of Kettle and Stony Point First Nation members approved a 90-million-dollar financial settlement with the Canadian government which included the return of land appropriated by the federal government in 1942 and the cleanup of Stony Point lands.

I went to the Stony Point Reserve in 2015 with Stacey. Being there brought back memories, to the time when I dispatched for the OPP and the fate of Dudley George.

Today, Stony Point is bleak, the original barracks from the 40's are dilapidated, yet people occupy these as their homes. It looked like a movie scene from *The Walking Dead* — abandoned cars, trailers and debris littered the grounds.

My eyes flashed through many scenes. I was numbed by what I saw.

Inside, I feel the continued struggle of the native people. I empathize with them and applaud them at the same time for their bravery in standing up for what was theirs in the first place.

I remember pulling up to a barrack where Stacey's friends lived. I remained in the vehicle, grieving the poverty around me.

We did this, the white man.

Coincidentally when I was a very young child, Mom and Dad would load all six of us up into the car (no seat belts in those days) and bring us on a summer vacation to Ipperwash (beach and cottages), which was adjacent to the previous Army Camp. The lands that were taken from the Native people decades ago, were turned into a tourist area.

I vaguely remember much, other than the name of our cottage rental called *Kinnikinnick*. There was sun, sand and playing on the beach. I remember a huge tub inside the cottage that I would fill and play in, feeling like I had my own pool.

Isn't it ironic, that the white man used the language of North American and First Nations to name their cottages? Kinnikinnick is a Native American and First Nations herbal smoking mixture, made from a traditional combination of leaves or barks. Recipes for the mixture vary, as do the uses, from social, to spiritual to medicinal.

If you are with people who make jokes about or voice distorted perceptions of other races, stand up and say something. Like bullying, if we just stand by and watch, we are in essence supporting the

Flaming-Torch Piñata Tip:

Stuff your young Piñatas with the truth, versus a distorted belief system that supports racism, division and fear. Parents can take the lead on this, by discussing the topic of racism with their children.

behavior of bullying. Cowards support bullying. People who have guts change the world. A young man in custody told me that I have more balls (guts) than most men. I do.

Have you immersed yourself in another culture to experience their differences and similarities? I had the opportunity to be wrapped in native culture and this was part of the master plan God created for me. Little did I know then, that this chapter in my life, was yet another lesson, preparing me for what was coming next.

Chapter Twenty-Five
Experiencing Native Culture

Since I began my relationship with Stacey, I have spent time on reserves in Ontario, attending Pow Wow's or other community functions. My eyes see the devastation of racism, the crumbling infrastructure in the communities and extreme poverty.

A movie called "*3rd World Canada*" was written, directed and produced by Andree Cazabon in 2010. The movie was filmed in a native reserve in Ontario — Kitchuhmaykoosib Inninuwug, following the suicide of three parents that left eight children orphaned. The documentary explores the impact of 3rd world conditions on this reserve, which is common in many reserves. www.thirdworldcanada.ca

Stacey – A Light of Hope

Stacey has a depth of spirituality, an appreciation for life, gratefulness and a connection to Creator (God) beyond any person I have ever met. I call him my angel. I asked Stacey what cloud he fell out of and he replied, "The one above you."

I've participated in a sweat lodge ceremony with him and others and felt the intensity of spiritual connectedness. The ceremony is held in a dome shaped structure made of tree saplings that are tied together. The structure is then covered with a canvas.

Inside the sweat, there is a circle dug in the center to hold the heated, hand selected rocks, pre-heated in fire at coal level.

I sat inside the sweat with Stacey, healers and elders. I felt blessed to be part of a ceremony I wouldn't have experienced had I not met him.

In part of the ceremony, the cover closes, and water is poured over hot rocks, producing steam. The participants sing traditional native songs, pray and share experiences of blessings and gratefulness for Creator and Mother Earth.

Sage, sweet grass, cedar and tobacco are considered plant medicines and used in the sweat lodge. Natives believe that plants give up their lives so that they can use their smoke for prayers and cleansing. The aroma produced by these plants in their dried state, helps them go into a different state of mind thus entering a deeper part of self. When they concentrate on what is happening in the moment, the scent may inspire memories, awaken the soul and give a sense of direction.

Many cultures and religions use sacred smoke made from the plant medicines. This is called smudging in First Nation and Native American culture. The aforementioned plants are burned during rituals, both for purification and to symbolize the prayers of the worshipper, which are then carried to the Creator along the smoke.

While much is written on the use of smudging to cleanse negative energy, one of its main purposes is to bring vision, aided by the sense of smell. Besides producing visions, smudging is used to purify tools and people before an important spiritual ceremony. It is also used to clear sacred space and open the soul before calling upon the Spirits and their healing powers.

Inside of the lodge, Stacey's piercing voice filled the sweat as he sang beautiful native songs. This palatable energy awakened my spirit and permeated my bones.

Hours into the ceremony, the cover of the sweat rose, just long enough to cool down and again, the cover dropped. Round two began.

I felt like I was melting, as balls of sweat rolled down my face and body. I debated giving up as the heat was nearly intolerable, yet I remained knowing that this is part of my journey — to step out of my comfort zone.

The healers spoke one by one as I transcended into a different world…. going back in time hundreds of years. I detached from this world and transported into timeless energy.

I gazed at the glowing red rocks and saw a bluish-purple hue (spirit energy) dancing above them — it was beautiful and mesmerizing.

I then saw myself as a native person. I was wearing full native regalia. It was me, but not me now. I was dancing wildly, without limitation. The colorful, bold feathers danced with me. I moved with joy and passion, my arms and feet flowed in perfect synergy.

A voice spoke to me, "You are free." It was my inner voice/connection to God. He spoke to me.

I felt liberated and disconnected from the other world across the bridge, where I came from. I was connected to Creator, to other spirits, the moon, the sky, the air and to Mother Earth. I was one with the people who allowed me access to a very personal, spiritual, sacred ceremony.

The sweat lasted for hours. We nestled in the cocoon surrounded by the crisp air of the winter night; under the stars connecting to Creator and the ancestors.

When we were done, we gathered at the house and had a feast of food. A sample of every food was placed in tree bark and a smudging ceremony followed, blessing the food and expressing gratitude to Creator for these gifts and revelations of the evening.

The sweat is a different experience for each person. Participants may get answers to things that are concerning them. Some share what they experienced and others choose to keep it within.

Stacey and the attending spiritual healers channeled information that flowed to them from Creator and the ancestors. Their bodies became a means of conducting great wisdom, healing, love, and gratitude. This is spirit in action at a glorious level that few get to witness, yet understand or believe.

The beauty of the native people was disturbed long ago. These *Spiritual Piñatas* are devoted to keeping their culture alive. They are trying to bring their people back to the time where they existed in their natural state.

Native communities, long before the European invasion, could be the model of perfection. There was sharing, love, faith, prayer, and nurturing of the young by every generation. A child was a community child, with each elder passing their gifts and knowledge to the young. Everything was done to the advantage of all.

Alcohol was introduced to the native people through European settlers in the early 1800's. Rum was used as trade by the Europeans to acquire fur from the natives. The sly traders knew that alcohol was a not a durable product; it would eventually run out and that the natives would want more.

This transaction of providing a drug (alcohol) to non-drug users, to get them hooked (for repeat business) reminds me of drug dealers today. The faster they get a person hooked, the higher their income.

Firstly, the natives did not have any experience with alcohol and its effects. Some may have believed that this altered state from drinking rum, may have placed them in contact with the world of spirits.

In order to achieve a natural altered state (pre-alcohol), the natives often fasted, or participated in sweat lodge rituals or vision quests. Intoxication may have originally meant not flight but search; not escape, but fulfillment; not loss of self, but discovery of self. To them it may have been intended as a positive, spiritual experience.

Alcohol spread through the native society because of the sense of power, lack of fear or expression that one felt under its influence.

Alcohol was taken in sufficient quantities to bring a state of complete intoxication. This sensation of invulnerability may have seemed attractive in a sense — especially in a culture where one's position was directly tied to strength and bravery.

From historical account, it would seem that when they drank, natives were liable to commit dangerous, reckless and violent acts. Keep in mind that these accounts came to us from the writings of Europeans, often accompanied with bias and unclear motivation.

There are accounts of Native Americans who consumed alcohol in moderation, yet the sharing of this information is simply not as numerous. The lack of alternative accounts has created a negative stereotype, with the drunken native as the norm.

Europeans had centuries of experience with alcohol. Natives, with no experience as to its effects, coupled with a large supply of potent alcohol, it's no surprise that Native communities were blindsided by the powerful results of drinking.

Another thing we can be quite certain of, is Native Americans are not the only group of people who, when their world was changing in dramatic ways, turned to alcohol as a way of coping.

Following the industrial revolution, alcohol consumption became far greater, as a way of dealing with a rapidly changing world.

Today, the world is changing at a rapid rate, through technology, global warming, instability and unease. The use of drugs as an escape, a means to cope, to abuse, has become a global problem. As I write this, governments in the USA and Canada are addressing a social crisis of Fentanyl related deaths.

I'd like to share with you my experiences on reserves, to give you a glimpse of what the long-term effects of racism and Residential Schools has done to the native people. In the next chapter, I paint a picture of their life and in spite of all they have endured, family and maintaining traditions are very important.

Chapter Twenty-Six
The Angel of Hope Piñata of Walpole Island

Today, it's numbing to see the domino effect of the Canadian Government's historical genocide of native communities. Many of the houses are very old, dilapidated, with leaking roofs and poor or no insulation.

While driving through the reservation I asked Stacey, "Do people live in that house?" totally shocked at what appeared to be life inside the torn remnants of what was once a home.

He replied "Yes, they do."

I asked, "Why?"

"That's the way it is," he said.

There is insufficient housing and the housing that is there, is poor. Several homes house two or three generations of families. There are a few nice houses, but the majority are run down.

Anytime I cross the bridge to the reserve, I am entering a different world — a community of people trying to cope with the residual effect of racism and centuries of lost culture.

Stacey is a beacon of hope and light on the reserve. He's a drug counselor, learning best about addiction from living through it with his family, and from his own personal experience.

Stacey has devoted his life to sobriety, to Creator, to his culture and guiding others in his community to a better life. I call him the energizer bunny as he keeps going and going and going. He has organized the community Pow Wow for years. He's teaching younger ones in the community about native culture, such as sewing moccasins and Pow Wow dancing. I call him, the *Mother Teresa* of Walpole Island. He touches people on a smaller scale, but it's done equally with love for mankind.

Stacey is extremely positive and never complains about anything. A lot of Piñatas need to be in his presence, just to learn about gratitude.

In the past, I must confess I wasn't truly grateful, and focused my worth on how much material stuff I had acquired. My measure of richness was largely about things. Having stuff was a way to show my value in the world.

I recall being stuffed with a feeling of lack in my childhood. That stuffing of lack kept me on edge with worry, anxiousness, making me blind to my own abundance. I worked physically harder and more hours to get ahead.

I often heard dreadful predictions of pending financial collapse, lay off's and economic downfall that was going to plummet us all into despair. If you had a job, you were lucky, even if you hated your job, you were lined up for a pension. A pension is security, if you are able to last until you are 55-65 years old. Taking the 9-5 type job typically included setting aside your talents and passions in exchange for a steady pay check.

I know my destiny is to speak and help others on earth, even if I have to give up the steady paycheck. I learned a lot of this by being in the presence of someone who lives like this daily.

Being with Stacey opened my eyes about basic human survival, living without excess or waste. I have transcended from needing things/security to be thankful. Stacey is also a grief counselor and sings, drums and leads prayer at funerals in his community. There is a sacred fire that is started for the passing spirit.

Stacey's sister passed away and the ceremonies included days of showing her body in her home, drumming, singing and prayers to celebrate her life. A teepee was set up beside her home, where a sacred fire burned inside, day and night until her burial.

Family and friends watched over the fire. Stacey built a ceremonial lodge with tree saplings beside the teepee. He did everything she asked him to do before she passed. He honored her wishes with love.

Stacey remained with her body overnight in the final celebrations, prior to her service the next morning. Her casket was placed in the back of a pickup truck and her sisters and female friends were the pall barriers. A service took place inside the community hall with Stacey officiating. Many gathered and shared in the ceremony, followed by a procession to the grave site.

At the cemetery, she was placed beside the grave where her body would rest for generations to come. With cloudy skies above and rain lurking, the sun broke through long enough to shine upon her service.

The sun was warm and as the rays struck the earth, steam floated above the ground. Stacey continued the dedication and prayers as mourners watched over. The pounding of the sacred drum rang through the stillness of the cemetery. The voices of native singers broke through the silence of death, celebrating her transition to the other side.

Coincidentally, two fighter jets from the American side, flew overhead. I thought, *Ah, perfect timing.* She is "leaving on a jet plane," on a direct one-way flight to heaven. I smiled inside. Colleen, like the rest of her siblings, lived a very difficult life. She seemed to be a pillar for many and a caretaker. She was worn and pulled in every direction. She experienced much loss. She was loved by many and loved many.

Mourners were asked to take tobacco and sage and throw it into her resting place. Her casket dropped as Stacey stood at the foot of her grave, singing from his heart, in his native language. The final dedication and the reality of her death overwhelmed him as tears poured down his face. His voice broke. She was gone.

She is free now — free of pain.

During the service, I stood helpless, watching Stacey overcome by grief, giving every ounce of his spirit to her. He looked like he was ready to drop to the earth, in complete emotional pain and exhaustion. He had not slept in days, making sure he fulfilled his sister's last wishes.

I just wanted to run over and hold him, but I would not interfere with his dedication of love. I was once again reminded of how special Stacey is; he's like no other man I have ever met in my life.

I stood in silence at the gravesite and watched mourners shovel dirt over her casket. It started to rain as the last few shovels of earth were thrown. People departed, one by one, to go back to the community center for a feast. I stood by Stacey as mourners moved along the procession, sharing their condolences with him and his family. I wondered how me, the little girl who once played on the sands of Ipperwash, was now standing on Native land and in a deep love relationship with Stacey. I also reflected on how my perception of the reserve had changed in my adulthood.

Years ago, when I was a dispatcher, I heard about all the violence and dysfunction in this native community. I can remember a large sign that stood just over the bridge as people entered the reserve, warning the OPP to stay out, with a picture of a gun. This was the residual effect of the death of Dudley George, a native who was shot and killed by an OPP officer, during a standoff with native protestors at Camp Ipperwash, which was eventually returned to the Chippewas of Kettle and Stony Point First Nation.

Land claims, high suicide rates and many social problems plague First Nations communities. The living conditions on most reserves are deplorable.

In March of 2016, nine people from one family died in a house fire on a remote Native Reserve in Canada's northern Ontario region. Three children and six adults died in the fire at Pikangikum First Nation.

The reserve had been in the news for a high number of suicides among young people and social problems. Canada's Native people face dire social and economic conditions, including poor housing.

The Canadian Press (2016) reported that homes in the community of 2,100 are overcrowded and in "outrageous disrepair," citing Joseph Magnet, a University of Ottawa law professor who has visited the reserve.

We have crushed the native people and their spirits. Lack of hope and cyclical abuse feeds alcoholism, drug abuse and suicide.

Stacey has little material things. Yet, he is wealthier than any millionaire I have ever met. He has something that is rare in this human world and cannot be purchased for any price. His spiritual stuffing is priceless and his depth of understanding of creation and gratitude for life is astonishing and authentic.

I feared this place long ago. I would not dare go there, for fear of being shot. That is what external stuffing told me about *them*.

But now, I realize though their world is much different than mine, we have much in common. I want to know more about them, help them, love them and be part of their healing and growth journey.

I wanted to be there the day Stacey was forced to bury his sister, but why did God ask *me* to experience this? Was I to be the link to share with the non-natives, the truth and plight of the North American Indian? Can *I* help be their voice?

God/Creator — Learning through Stacey about Spiritual Stuffing

Knowing Stacey has deepened my spirituality and awareness, he's provided a lot of new, healing stuffing — as good guides do. There is no greater gift than a trusting, grateful, and beautiful connection to Creator. Someone who shows you a new appreciation for life and earth, unspoiled by commercialism.

When we first met, I asked Stacey who God was to him. He called God, Creator. He said gracefully and beautifully with joy, "He is in the wind, in the stars, in the sky, in the grass." He went on to speak about Creator and connected instantly with my spirit. I knew he was different than any man I had met.

I grew up in the Catholic religion and it felt more like an obligation — a type of programming. A large part of the ceremony was repetition, leading to a robotic response, rather than an intent focus to purposely consume and learn from every word.

The Catholic Piñata's assembled into the seats of the church, all dressed up in their Sunday best. The Catholic Priest opened and closed the ceremony with predictable words and actions, such as kneeling or standing. Growing up, I felt guilt at times about being *bad* and I feared going to hell.

My *Children Piñatas* did not want to go to church, so much so that they would always manage to create a distraction by poking at each other during mass. Lisa was especially not interested in church. I'd get her all dolled up, wearing a beautiful dress, little white gloves, with a matching white purse and hat. She kicked and cried when the white dress shoes went on and would defiantly kick them off while sitting in the pew. Oh, the trauma I put these kids through!

My religion lacked the beauty of *open* heartfelt expression, love and communicating deeply with God. It lacked connection with earth.

I disliked the fact that the priest — a man, sat in a prominent position above of, or in front of, female nuns. It was a setting of perceived rank and superiority. This rank-stuffing brought out the women's activist in me at an early age. I felt that woman and men should be equal. I often wondered why a woman could not be a priest.

Along with congregation, I made the sign of the Cross through a symbolic motion. I touched my forehead, as I stated out loud, "In the name of the Father," then touched the lower middle of my chest, saying, "And of the Son," and then to my left shoulder, "Holy," and finally to the right shoulder with the word "Spirit."

I really didn't understand what spirit was, until I went through many falls. It took pain to understand my spirit. I had to go through hell to get to heaven.

God has a way of teaching us. When a situation in your life appears to be a loss, there is likely a hidden gift that you are unaware of. Through your life experiences, if you learned where you needed to evolve, learn and forgive — you are moving in the right direction.

I came to believe in God and feel the presence of spirit through *a knowing*, a much different experience than the programming from my Catholic upbringing. I call it programming, as there is a significant difference when our stuffing comes from a place of human perspective versus Godly origin.

Stacey helped me return to golden memories that I had not felt since childhood, through reconnecting me to Mother Earth. We laid in the grass — talked, giggled and felt joyful looking up to the sky and trees. A child-like, feel-so-good stuffing returned. It was wonderful to touch the blades, smell the air, and see the birds and all without worry, a to-do list, or agenda.

I felt a peace within me that was severed long ago. Growing up, and being sculpted by the adult rat race, a concrete world and media splatter, detached me from inner peace, joy and smelling the clean air. These worldly adaptations caused me to look outward instead of inward.

Chapter Twenty-Seven
A Piñata Love Story and the Good Luck Praying Mantis

I sat in church one day and Pastor Brad asked the congregation, "What do you need to let go of?"

I thought about all the therapy I had gone through to discover why I chose the men that I did, which ultimately turned out to be unsuccessful for all involved.

I always felt that if I did not have *someone in my life*, then I wasn't good enough, beautiful enough, and smart enough. This was my Piñata's low self-esteem stuffing to the nines.

A Piñata needs to understand that self-love is the beginning of healthy relationships with others.

I remember thinking (and talking to God), in response to Pastor Brad's question — *God, I don't need a man in my life to make me happy and complete. I need to let go of this belief. I trust that at the right time You will bring the right person to me, to be part of my life. Besides God, I have really messed up in that department!*

I had to stop *looking* for a mate and be satisfied being alone, spending time with Charlene, doing the things that brought me happiness. It was hard in the beginning, because I was not used to being alone. But ultimately, I let go of my fleshly desires and trusted in God.

A few months later, Stacey fell out of a cloud in Heaven. Not literally.

We were on a professional networking site called *LinkedIn*. Stacey viewed my profile and sent me a message, saying how he could sense my wonderful spirit through my words and the things I had done. I thought that was nice, and decided to read his profile.

I resonated with the similarities in our individual interests — drug abuse prevention, music, community work and family. I called him my twin and he thought that was funny. We decided to meet a week later and that moment changed his and my life. I saved every message we sent to each other.

We often spoke about how grateful we were to God in bringing us together. We'd make the OK sign with our hands and look up to the sky and say together, "Thank you, Creator."

One of our favorite words was "Yaaaymen" which is a combination of the expression, Yaaay, blended with amen.

In the early stages of our relationship, it felt like we knew each other forever. Stacey wrote in September of 2014, "I have the same feeling of knowing you forever and so accepting of this eternal sense that comes from the soul's energy. Finding you, was put in place a long time ago when I wondered when I would love someone like I want to. A love that allows for fireflies, butterflies, trembling, shaking, quivering, yearning, dreaming, resting, playing, believing, freeing, pleasuring, laughing, empowering, and doing it all over again daily. Isn't that an amazing journey?"

I'd say, "Yes Stacey, it is amazing." My younger self would likely have agreed.

The Vision of the Praying Mantis

A long time ago when I was about five years old, I was playing outside and saw a praying mantis *the size of our house*, leaning against the roof, as though it was praying over the people inside. I started screaming and ran into the house and warned everyone about the monster-sized praying mantis that was leaning on the roof. I screamed in fear thinking the roof would cave in at any moment.

Everyone ran outside and lo and behold, there was nothing, it was "just Charlene" and her imagination.

Many years later, I researched the significance of what this sighting could represent. Some cultures see the praying mantis as a good luck omen.

Fast forward — forty-five years later. Stacey was at my house and I was barbecuing in the back yard.

I saw a praying mantis in the tree and pointed it out to him. We looked at the interesting insect. Stacey decided to go to his truck and get his camera to take a picture. I walked back in the house with the cooked food and at the same time, Stacey was walking into the house from the front door. As he opened the door and walked in, a praying mantis flew in with him. I could not believe my eyes.

I said, "Look," and of course, Stacey, without hesitation, picked the mantis up. He wanted to give me a close-up view. He pointed it at me held between his fingers.

I squealed, "Put that thing down, it will bite you!"

He laughed and said, "It won't bite!"

I said, "Is that the same praying mantis that was in the tree in the back yard?"

We walked outside and the praying mantis in the tree was still there. Two praying mantises in less than ten minutes, when I had not seen one on my property ever.

I told Stacey about the gigantic praying mantis that I'd seen years ago. I asked him what he felt a praying mantis symbolized and he said "luck". We just smiled.

We continuously reminded each other how lucky we were that we found each other, and expressed gratitude.

Sparkling Piñata Tips about LOVE stuffing:

- Love is being kind, loving and supportive of each other.
- Love is letting the other do things that bring them joy, without making them feel guilty.
- Love is thoughtful words and actions. When you love another, it is joyful to do things for them, because you care about them.
- Love doesn't happen through picking up a guy or gal at the local bar and going home to roll in the hay. That's sex.
- Love isn't conditional, example: You need to do a, b, c and d, then I will love you. That's a false distortion of love based on a wish list or conditions. This has a self-centered focus. When you truly love someone, love is the foundation to build upon."
- Love is spending quality time together.
- Love is trust and communication.
- Love is sharing affection through physical touch, intimacy and looking into each other's eyes and smiling.
- Love is equality in a relationship and balancing responsibilities.

Chapter Twenty-Eight
Collaborating with The Universe

When you were young, what did you dream about becoming when you grew up? A firefighter, a policeman/woman, a parent, a singer, an actress? What was it?

Do you remember when you laid in the grass, looked up to the sky and gazed at countless, beautiful stars? I bet you looked for the big and little dipper too. Did these experiences bring you joy? Did you feel at peace?

When I was about nine years old, I laid in the grass on a hill with my cousin Rachelle. We would gab for hours and talk about our dreams and my annoying brothers. I lived on a farm and being outside enjoying nature and animals was a blessing. Rachelle came from the city, so the farm was quite the adventure for her.

I loved the sunshine, jumping in the mud with my barn boots and playing with the kittens in the barn. It was very peaceful being outdoors, except for when I played my clarinet and my dog Lady instantly howled.

I remember telling Rachelle, while gazing up at the white fluffy clouds, against the blue sky, that I wanted to be on a stage one day, speaking, singing and helping thousands of people. As these words rolled out of my mouth, my mind pictured me standing there, on stage, with a microphone in my hand, looking out to the crowd and speaking to them. I don't know what I was telling them, but many were smiling.

Rachelle and I would play in the corn crib on the farm — standing on a wagon pretending we were stars, singing to a crowd of people. We each held a corncob, pretending it was our microphone. Rachelle's mom — my Aunt Carol, was my inspiration to become a singer. She was a talented country singer in a band.

Many years later, my dreams actualized. I sang at hundreds of events and became a professional speaker with the Canadian Association of Professional Speakers.

I had a goal in late high school to become a police officer. I am a Special Constable (not a police officer, but a peace officer) and have policed for twenty-four years, doing various jobs.

I never felt that policing was the best match for my talents and personality. I was the square peg trying to fit into a round hole. No matter how hard I tried *to fit in*, I didn't mirror the conventional cop-type model. And, it didn't matter to me if I fit in. I was me. It wasn't that I didn't do a very good job or worked hard. I knew that my best talents of creativity, singing, event organizing, and public speaking, weren't collectively used in policing.

While working full time and raising my family, I continued to pursue my dreams of singing and speaking. These were natural to me and activities that connected me with hundreds of people, allowing me to express my spirit. I know that if you or I keep stepping towards our goals/dreams, with commitment, passion and diligent efforts, that the universe will step in to assist us.

The Universe in Action

For years, I suffered from depression, then fibromyalgia, most in part from the stress caused by unhealthy relationships. I was also under tremendous stress (which affected my mental health and activated my fibromyalgia) because of bullying by co-workers and the strain of rebuilding from debris after my psychosis. With health issues caused solely by my day job, I went home after work completely exhausted. I considered giving up my speaking, as I did not have an ounce of spare energy. My diagnosis of adrenal fatigue magnified my issues.

In fall of 2016, I was approached by Jim Lutes and Jim Britt about being a co-author in *The Change*, a series of books focused on empowerment, inspiration and personal growth. I had at this time, already began to write a full book, the one you are holding — *The Piñata Theory™*.

With no experience or background as an author, I felt it was wise to be under the wing and talents of these experienced, successful mentors. Both Jim's had achieved great status in speaking, coaching, writing and business training, around the world.

I had an opportunity to be a co-author in book twelve of *The Change*, by contributing one chapter called *The Piñata Theory™*. It was the condensed version of my philosophy. I felt this would be a positive stepping stone prior to writing a full book; connecting me with amazing authors, coaches, speakers and wellness experts around the world. And, it did. Today, I have close friendships and collaborations with co-authors as a result.

When I was tossing around the thought of giving up on my professional speaking because of my health, I consulted with two exceptional speakers who were part of my local speaking association — the Canadian Association of Professional Speakers, Southwestern Ontario. I shared with Bob Parker and Greg Schinkel, the obstacles that I was facing and also wondered when to break out with my story. I contacted each individually and waited for a response.

Bob and Greg gave me many things to think about, both offering realistic points. Greg encouraged me to stay on, as he said that the group valued my participation. Bob said that before I told my story, I needed to have the stamina to ride the wave once it started to roll, meaning, was I ready mentally and physically?

I also had to ask how this choice would affect my relationships. Stacey supported and encouraged me, so I wasn't concerned about us. I often shared my writing with him, especially since he was part of the book. Stacey would sit and listen as I read and he smiled.

My children are grown and independent, so the need for child-rearing had passed. Lisa and Jordan were also very supportive of me. I did my best to encourage both of them to go after their dreams and follow the wisdom of their heart.

I told Bob I would leave it up to the universe to provide me with an answer. I knew the time had come to stop straining over it. I asked the universe and let it be.

The very next day I headed down to the local *Tea Connection* store. I needed to pick up herbal teas that my Natural Path recommended.

While filling my tea order, I chatted with a few of the customers in the store. One worked with CTV news and he was recently at my workplace covering an important case. We also talked about the temporary wall that was erected at the storefront. A car drove through the front window of the store, one evening, causing sizable damage.

While I stood waiting my turn, I read a poster about a tea cup reader (Stella) who provided her services at the store. I inquired and discovered that she was working. Stella walked over and introduced herself. She said the readings were on special, with the proceeds donated towards the cost of a new storefront. I thought what the heck, it was for a good cause.

Stella asked me to select a tea and I chose peppermint. Julie prepared a cup and I sat down on a chair and sipped away, leaving just a sprinkle of moisture on the leaves.

"Ok, I think it's good," I said to Stella as I looked down at the soggy tea leaves.

Stella and I proceeded to sit down in a corner near a plant, for my reading. Stella had wonderful energy that I immediately sensed. She said that she was a fourth-generation tea cup reader. I thought this was quite intriguing — this talent must be part of her DNA-Stuffing.

Stella looked intently at the leaves at the bottom of the cup. She *saw* things. I was amazed by how she would focus on a spot inside the cup, like she was observing something in vivid detail, which she did. Stella giggled when she saw something funny.

Stella told me I was at a crossroads in my life and that both paths were good for me. The universe was answering my question, less than twelve hours later!

I listened intently to what was next. Stella saw me sitting in front of a computer. She also saw a book and a pen on the table to the right of the computer. She felt that the emphasis was on the writing, rather than the computer.

Stella told me I have many guides helping me here on earth and they are on guard, anxious for me to ask for help. I felt reassured knowing I had a team of invisible helpers. I always knew I did. I believe in guides and angels and that every person has them to help in their earthly journey. The key to getting them actively engaged is simple — just ask for help and boom, they are on it.

Stella told me many things and asked me if I worked on the radio. I said no, but I have been a guest on the radio several times. Stella saw me (yep, in the tea leaves) sitting in front of a microphone in a studio talking about something. She vividly described things, as though she was holding a picture instead of a cup.

Stella smiled and burst into a giggle. Her giddiness was contagious and joyful — it came from the heart. Stella made me chuckle each time she found something special in the tea cup.

She continued, "Okay, they are showing me now. Your guides are telling me that you need to write a book!"

Stella literally saw a book "*glowing*" to which she affirmed, "You are writing a book." When the guides want to make a point, they don't mess around.

I had not told Stella that I was writing a book. I smiled.

Stella also saw me at a book signing event and people were lined up. She said it would happen quite quickly and that *I needed to be ready* as Bob indicated to me *the night before.*

She said, "This may sound odd, but, long ago when you were a child you put an intention out to the universe. This dream is going to come true."

I thought back to the time on the hill with Rachelle and knew this was the exact moment my words and thoughts floated to the heavens, making my dream-maker guides jump for joy.

I gave Stella a big hug and told her I was writing a book. She screamed and of course giggled from the bottom of her toes this time. I thanked her for the insight and assured her, she indeed had a gift.

I explained to Stella that I was at a crossroads, and how I put the question out to the universe the evening before. I later shared with Stacey and my son Jordan, about the tea adventure and how my angels gave me the message I needed to hear. It was affirmation from the universe.

Chapter Twenty-Nine
The Unseen Spirit World

Why do you need to know my story? Because, I'm living proof that much more exists than what we see.

Are *You* in a difficult circumstance right now? Are you feeling stuck in a situation that doesn't fulfill you, or facing a crossroad in your life?

If you do not believe in coincidences and questions answered, I encourage you to try communicating with the universe or with God or with your angels.

Remember to be open-minded and trusting of help from above. You also must believe in the extraordinary, and a presence with us every day, that you cannot touch or see.

Some Piñatas are as skeptical as Scrooge, and claim, "Bah, humbug! If you cannot see or touch something, *it* just isn't real." I am telling you right now that *it* is.

Since an early age, I have seen, felt and heard things... experiences that shouldn't happen, according to the normal world.

I had an out-of-body experience years ago while lying in bed and reported back to someone who lived ten miles away, what I saw in their house that morning, without physically being there. This person later confirmed my experience.

I have heard the scream of the devil and seen silhouettes of spirits (including my ex's wife, who committed suicide) walk through my house. One spirit came before I had guests coming for an angel circle. I told the spirit that she was early, and the party was starting at 7:00 p.m.

That evening, a guest at my gathering fell outside of the house when she left. She later told me that *something* pushed her. She felt dark energy in the home that night. At that time, I was going through horrible experiences with my step-children.

I also saw the spirit outline of my missing cat Milo that night. It was confirmation that he died. My ex's children constantly encouraged their cat to attack Milo. One day he was gone, without explanation.

Years prior, I remember laying in bed sobbing about a failed relationship. While crying and speaking to God, I kept asking, *Why me?* I felt something wrap around my body and hold me. I stopped crying and felt peace. It was incredible.

Once, I was driving along a beautiful rural roadway that was near trees, fields and farm animals. I saw a dead raccoon on the road and prayed for him, feeling sadness about his traumatic death. He had obviously been hit by a car. I prayed for his little spirit and thanked him for his life on earth.

As I prayed, a loud voice said, "Hit the brakes!"

Without hesitation, I stomped on the brake of my Ford Escape and watched in complete shock as a buck deer leaped across the front of my truck. This beautiful animal with enormous antlers, sailed across the windshield in front of me, in what seemed, super slow, slide by slide motion. I barely missed him, by a millisecond.

I sat there stunned and in disbelief with my vehicle completely stopped on the roadway. I was grateful for the voice that warned me of impending danger. I knew that the spirit of the raccoon heard my prayers and reciprocated by protecting me and the deer.

I was never afraid of any of these experiences, as I believed in God, the spiritual realm and angels.

Connection to the Divine

In order to connect with the unseen, we need to go back to a child-like state that existed before we were overloaded and weighed down with belief stuffing. This particular stuffing, likely did not encourage you to believe in things you couldn't see. Although you may have received religious teaching about God or the angels or the devil (unseen entities), odds are great you likely did not receive instruction on how to communicate with God, angels or the universe at school.

As children, we dreamed with expectation...largely absent of doubt, fear, worry and how-to stuffing. As you read this, think about your dreams, maybe dreams that were parked long ago. I encourage you to take one item from your dream-list and go for it. Take the necessary steps to achieve that goal, one day at a time. The end product or result may take time, however, focus on and enjoy the process. This is the beauty of goals or dreams...the experience along the way.

Believe without fear, worry or hesitation that the universe will line up events or people for you, once you start using your gifts and talents in a passionate, benevolent, and joyful way.

Now, get your Piñata feet moving. Some Piñatas want to do things, yet don't invest the time or effort needed, before giving up or letting their dreams slide.

Don't sit on your Piñata butt and think a treasure or talent is going to fall from the sky while you are on sitting on the couch into your third hour of television. To be successful in a desired venture, business, hobby, relationship or study, a Piñata must engage in regular, intentional and conscious actions to support the activity or cause. Once we do, events will unfold for us, even if we don't have all the of the resources, answers or know what's next.

Our actions are best rewarded when we serve God, humanity and our spirit. If someone wants to learn to sing, solely to make money or to become famous, they are missing the point of the art. Also, some Piñatas believe that other Piñatas had the advantage of being born with a skill or are naturally gifted. Piñatas who are very good at something, did a lot of hard work to get where they are. They fell, got discouraged, but got moving again. They didn't give up or make up excuses.

A Piñata should engage in an activity, because it brings their spirit joy — it awakens the artist within, bursts their creativity and fires up the brain cells. When a Piñata awakens their spirit, and listens to their inner GPS — their life becomes fulfilled beyond what they ever expected or imagined.

When you are engaged in the things you enjoy doing, along the way you will meet someone who will be part of your life, in a minor or significant way. A friend of mine hosted karaoke shows and met the love of her life at a karaoke event. Her now husband Marty, was dropping his kids off at the club, as they wanted to sing. He had no intention of staying and was still wearing his dirty clothes from work-ing on the farm. Marty decided to go in for only a few minutes, until he set eyes on Carrie. He was just blown away by her presence. They married the next year.

Carrie had some very good advice for me when I attended her wedding solo, stating, "Charlene, don't look," referring to looking for a relationship. "Just do what you do and he will come." One year later, when I wasn't looking, Stacey came into my life.

Don't let age deter you from taking up a new hobby or trying some-thing new.

Anna Mary Robertson Moses, known as Grandma Moses, began painting intensely at the age of 78. She had not taken an art lesson in her life. She picked up a brush, paint and a canvass and away she went.

She had no idea that her new hobby would change her life and inspire a nation.

Grandma Moses displayed her art at a local general store. One day an art dealer happened to be driving through and stopped. He was flabbergasted at the art and asked the clerk, "Who painted all of these?"

The clerk replied, "Grandma Moses," and told the man she lived nearby.

The art dealer got in his car and had to meet this amazing artist. The rest is history. Her works have been shown and sold in the United States and abroad and have been marketed on greeting cards and other merchandise. Moses' paintings are among the collections of many museums. Her painting, *The Sugaring Off,* was sold for US$1.2 million in 2006.

Her story is a perfect example about how doing what you love will create a ripple effect in the universe. In the next chapter, we'll talk about the things holding us back and how to overcome them.

Chapter Thirty
Don't Let Another Piñata Hold You Back!

In 2012, the police service I am employed with, took my job position away and placed me in another role. Regardless of the lives I helped, and the phenomenal work I did in the schools and community, they saw me as no longer needed. Because of the psychotic stress reaction resulting from the abuses I endured in my last marriage, I faced domestic charges. The powers that be, handled me like a violent criminal instead of an abused woman who had hit rock bottom.

I was ultimately given an Absolute Discharge by the Judge, resulting in no criminal record. The Judge made it clear, that it would be a disservice to the public to remove me from my role in the schools and community. I had twenty-five reference letters from educators, politicians, family, friends, and people in law enforcement and from committees I served on, supporting my character and exceptional passion in helping others.

What happened to me was a very bizarre and extreme event. I felt like Farrah Fawcett's character, in the movie, *The Burning Bed*.

The movie is based on a true story, about Francine Hughes, (Michigan, USA). A woman who was abused by her drunken husband for thirteen years. One night, after he raped and beat her, he passed out drunk in bed.

Francine told her four children to go sit in the car. She then poured gasoline around the bed that her husband slept in and set it on fire, resulting in his death. She was found not guilty of murder charges, due to temporary insanity.

This is extreme and totally different from my case, however, the base of her mental state resulted from ongoing abuse. My abuse was emotional and mentally inflicted upon me by my ex and his offspring.

His children were tactful and ruthless in their joint efforts to destroy me.

After the mental meltdown, I went under the care of a psychologist, psychiatrist and my family doctor. All three professionals concurred that the incident was situational, and specifically due to the abuse in my home environment.

I believe that my mind went into "fight or flight" crisis mode that fateful night. My built-in *Piñata Survival Instinct* took control, fighting for my life. I predict that I would have been dead, in time, had this psychotic event not happened. This life-changing moment freed me of this horrible environment, against my conscious will, because I would have continued to try to make it work. I was addicted to fixing and not equipped to handle such highly dysfunctional people. It was time to take care of my Piñata. She was broken. But, not for long.

This event was blessing in disguise, because it got me out of that dreadful marriage and saved my life.

I found a great legal team, including my divorce lawyer Tamara Stomp. She kept me grounded through the drama and protected my rights. Tamara helped me navigate out of this nightmare and encouraged me every stop of the way.

I asked Tamara how I could continue speaking after what happened. She said, *"Charlene, you were an abused woman. Go tell your story, help others."*

I was determined to reach my dreams of speaking, regardless of my employer's decision to remove me from my public service position.

I knew what I was made of and more so, what I am capable of. The story was not going to end there. It was the turning point — my launch into destiny.

People and situations will put roadblocks in your way. Reroute, just like your GPS does when the road is closed or there's heavy traffic. Find a way. Don't focus on them or the situation, focus on your goals and keep those feet moving…forward.

For years, I was trapped in a mason jar with the lid screwed on tight. That's what happens when we allow other Piñatas to drive our bus or allow our subconscious mind or ego to be in charge.

Piñata Power – Let Your Best Stuffing Shine!

- *Do not allow others to define you or control your destiny.*
- *Accept that some situations are best left as is, because it's fruitless to continue. Consider who the players are. If they are set in their ways, are ego driven or have personal agendas — even if you score on them or win, you will lose.*
- *Walk away with your head held high versus challenging a machine you know will make your life difficult or create roadblocks.*
- *Get your game on — shake the dust off your stuffing and get up!*
- *You have gifts and talents that make you feel awesome, that come naturally. Keep doing what brings you joy and blesses others.*
- *Pray. Forgive. Learn. Move Forward.*

As I write this, I am happy to report I made it through the messiness of the past, and today I know that God had a plan in all of this. I have an opportunity to encourage people with addictions and those facing major problems in their lives. I am able to speak to people to help them, to make a difference, by referring them to addiction programs, mental health programs, talking about God, and giving them encouragement not to give up. I know I have impacted many, and for this I thank God for putting me here.

Here's another Sparkling Piñata Tip for you.

These sprinkles are red, as in STOP.

People will try to stop you by veiled threats or by putting a stone ahead of your wheels, because you challenge injustices. Tell your Piñata to stand up to them, because, the people who do, make changes in the world. Be the Mother Teresa or the Rosa Parks of your generation. Remember the stuffing you are made of. You will not cower to bullies! Stand up for your rights. Yet, be careful as some battles are best to walk away from. Your sanity, your time, your dignity, your safety and your health are paramount.

One-on-One Piñata Talk

If you are in an unhealthy relationship that causes you illness, physical or mental abuse, you seriously need to protect yourself and literally fight for your life. Completely remove yourself from the source of your pain, especially if there are children involved. Remember, our little Piñatas download everything they see, hear and experience.

If you are in an unhealthy relationship and wish to see if there is hope for change, then distance yourself first from the abuser, then set up counseling. The distance creates clarity, without interference or pressure. If the other partner is serious about working on the issues, they will do so, knowing you will no longer accept the status quo.

If you are in a work environment that is toxic — such as bullying, harassment, or racism, you need to report to management what is happening. Keep a log of dates and times and words and actions. If you don't have the exact date, you can summarize approximate times the events happened, such as, September, 2015.

If you are represented by a union, make sure you report the

incidents to them. If there is no remedy by your employer, or through your union, civil litigation and other options are available to help you, such as human rights codes and labor laws.

Life is too short to stay in an unsatisfying job. However, in some instances sacrifices must be made in order to provide the essentials of life. In the meantime, keep broadening your horizons and expand your knowledge in the area that interests you. Set up a short-term and long-term plan of where you want to be, and keep focused.

While working, continue to live through spirit and look for opportunities to bless others. We may not be in the job we want today, but every day is a day to shine, to spread gratefulness, support, be complimentary to others and contribute to the team.

Thank and acknowledge the contribution of everyone in your company or organization. Check your ego at the door. Employees do best when they are valued, appreciated and included in decisions. It is important to encourage participation, learning and having a leader who is not a Piñata-Prick. I've had too many of those and it makes everyone's day miserable.

Well beyond the challenges of difficult people, exist deeply disturbed persons with extreme views or agendas, who threaten peace and security anytime, anywhere. I call them the *Piñata of Darkness*, and will explain why in the next chapter.

Chapter Thirty-One
The Piñata of Darkness

The *Piñata of Darkness*, or POD, does not fear or work for God. It's an evil entity that has taken over the mind, completely. The beautiful spirit that is within this Piñata is covered in thick, deep darkness. I believe in some cases the spirit has left.

This angry, evil, distorted, violent, vengeful or hateful stuffing exists in terrorists, serial killers, mass murderers and people who assassinate or willfully abuse others for their selfish gain.

This Piñata is void of love and will create a distorted reality to support their claim, cause or actions. They often learned hate from a very young age.

They were outsiders who didn't fit, often segregated, excluded, or bullied. Their silent anger grew and grew. Society provided them with plenty of violent TV shows and video games to learn how to kill. Lack of access to guns and weapons was not a barrier to their agenda.

The POD downloaded stuffing that supported superiority, racism, or hatred. They became desensitized to violence, abuse, and dysfunction, perhaps as a direct result of their family dynamics or social influences. They believe they are justified in inflicting and enforcing social justice. Some POD use distorted views of God to justify their acts of hate and violence.

Think about ISIS terrorists and their evil actions; beheading people, killing innocent human beings, suicide bombers, all avenues of complete mind distortion. Where is a single grain of love, light or truth in any of this? This is evil to the extreme. I feel that Satan (The Ruler of Darkness) has downloaded hate into them.

How do we *unstuff* this darkness from these Piñatas? I honestly think this is impossible. These people's minds and spirits have been overtaken and hijacked by the anti-spirit.

The only way to overcome evil is to build the team of God's followers and angels on earth. We shall overcome darkness with light.

This world is in the worst shape ever, and I honestly feel we are on the brink of dramatic global change. We will either die in global war or choose to work together, to survive.

Or, Mother Earth will step in and show us what we have done to her. We have exploited, damaged, and broken her. She has sat back with patience, hoping we'd understand her role in our existence and her powerful forces. In 2017, violent hurricanes ravaged the USA and the Caribbean Islands. Earthquakes shook Mexico, one after the other. She's literally slapping us in the face, saying, "Wake up!" I don't know what else she can do to force us to change.

Each of us has the responsibility to begin a spiritual journey, now. This means letting go of the ways of the flesh (lust, greed, excessive commercialism, ego, materialism, control, exploiting animals and the planet) and working toward bringing others to the light and teaching them the Word of God. Every human being has the moral responsibility to stop the growing wave of hate, through love. Our future and the future of our children, is in your hands and mine. Today — not tomorrow — today.

The next chapter helps Piñatas see the importance of living for the higher good, rather than doing our own will, in a selfish, often careless way. In your life you may have accumulated *Bullshit Stuffing*. This stuffing is buried deep within the subconscious mind, often the result of learned self-preservation or behavior from childhood. Yet, in adulthood this BS stuffing causes pain to you or other Piñatas.

Chapter Thirty-Two
Bullshit and Me-Agenda Stuffing: Avoiding Truth, Inviting Pain

Some Piñatas pretend to be happy or cover up the truth, to avoid admitting they have made a poor decision. Instead of paying attention to the signs and flags waving wildly at them, (universe and their spirit hoping to catch their attention), they discard the truth in order to get what they want. This is *Me-Agenda Stuffing* coupled with *BS-Stuffing*.

I am guilty of following my emotions, versus responding to the obvious, such as remaining in or entering into a relationship with someone who is irresponsible or not as devoted as I was. It felt good to be noticed, to be loved, to help, so the *Me-Agenda Stuffing* was part of the reason for sticking it out.

Bullshit-Stuffing (BS-Stuffing), is avoiding facts and doing it any- way, or creating a false reality to cover the truth, to make situations look better than they actually are. *Me-Agenda Stuffing* is often the launch pad for *BS-Stuffing*. *Me-Agenda Stuffing* is self-satisfying, done without honest evaluation or concern for long-term consequences, or both. Eventually these scenarios backfire and cause pain to someone.

BS-Stuffing is automatically working when we dismiss facts, in order to get what we want. *BS-Stuffing* covers up, makes excuses, pretends and is untruthful. Sometimes the motive is to avoid being judged by others, when a poor decision goes south.

See if you can identify the *BS-Stuffing* and *Me-Agenda Stuffing* in this example.

Joan is married to Gary. During their engagement, he cheated on Joan *several times*, yet she chose to marry him, thinking it would put an end to his cheating ways, believing commitment would change this. Joan blames his drinking on the cheating, thinking he truly loves her. Joan believes she has been too hard on Gary, no wonder he strayed. Joan did not tell her friends or family that Gary was cheating prior to the marriage.

Gary has cheated again during their marriage. Joan chooses to pretend everything is okay, not telling anyone. They attend events together and no one knows the truth. Joan finally has enough, after counseling attempts proves futile and decides to leave Gary.

This is Joan's *BS-Stuffing*, she is avoiding the plain truth and creating excuses for Gary's behavior, sometimes even blaming herself. Joan also covers up for Gary, so her friends and family don't find out about his double dipping. Yuck.

This is her *Me-Agenda Stuffing*. Joan chose to avoid the truth and create a false reality to get what she wanted — to be with Gary. This was short term vision, without careful consideration of how this would affect her long-term.

This is Joan's reality, she settled for trouble. Her *Me-Agenda Stuffing* backfired and the BS got deeper.

When Gary returned to his cheating after the marriage, Joan was *devastated*. Really Joan? Wake up and focus on the truth. Gary is a cheater and not even Joan could reel in this bad boy. Gary needs help, because he lies to people and thinks it's acceptable.

Joan experienced further pain and asked, *Why me?*

Unfortunately, Joan has low self-esteem stuffing; otherwise she would not have continued the relationship with Gary when he cheated on her during their engagement.

As my Aunt Helen always said, "If it walks like a duck and looks like a duck, it's a duck."

People can talk, talk, talk, but watch what they do. The truth eventually surfaces. A duck can pretend to be an eagle, for a while, but only the mighty eagle can truly be an eagle.

When an unhealthy relationship ends — count your lucky stars that you figured him/her out. Cut your *perceived losses* and have the self-love to move on!

When we cover up situations with *BS-Stuffing*, by avoiding the truth, eventually pain will result. Guaranteed.

I was like Joan — I saw all the flags, yet I chose to marry him anyway, hoping things would change.

Relationship Math 101 — What My Psychologist Taught Me

The psychologist appointed by the police, asked me to take a factual look at the relationship I was in. She really made me see the duck. The duck would never be an eagle.

The *truth* was, only 20% of the relationship was good and 80% was not. I was *hoping* that the 20% would grow into 80%. That's BS thinking. What you see is what you get and it's pretty self-explanatory. If you think he or she will change, especially after having a baby, moving, or getting married, you are full of Bullshit-stuffing. Had I accepted that he was an absolute fraud instead of listening to his lies, I would have saved myself a lot of grief.

Regardless of the façade some Piñatas create about a relationship, the body will tell us the truth and the facts will catch up to us. When we are in stressful, non-ethical or abusive relationships, our bodies will send us signs that we are living outside of wellness and in opposition of spirit. For months, before my psychogenic stress reaction, my body was screaming in pain from fibromyalgia. That was my red flag waving.

More Relationship Drama and BS-Stuffing:

Brittany Piñata (BP) broke up with Joey Piñata (JP) several times because of his behavior towards her. JP continued to call, text, and go to BP's house, begging her to get back together. He pleaded things would change. BP finally agreed, with hesitation, and started dating JP again.

BP was essentially avoiding the truth with BS-Stuffing. BP and JP dated on and off for four years. They both should have been mature, accepted the facts, knowing that this relationship was not healthy or fulfilling to either. It was evident that they were not compatible, nor did they share equal values.

Within weeks of being together again, JP returned to his old ways toward BP. Only this time it was much worse. They broke up again. The drama wheel was spinning out of control. What a soap opera! Brittany cried, Oops I did it again. Joey and Brittany, get your stuffing together!

If you are falling into relationships with unhealthy people that means you have some unhealthy stuffing to clean up.
Get some professional help and straighten up your stuffing.
When a relationship is over, take the time to examine all views in a truthful way.
Look at your part in the real-life play - were you the lead role, bystander, enabler, drama starter, insecure, too nice?

There are healthy people in healthy relationships all around us. I am always so happy to see a loving couple who have their stuffing together. These Piñatas stand out. Bravo!

They have a lot to feel thankful for, and as we'll discover next, this is a real secret to joy and happiness.

Chapter Thirty-Three
Gratefulness Stuffing

The more *Gratefulness Stuffing* that we download and ultimately share, the happier and more satisfied we will be. To be grateful means to feel or show an appreciation of anything in your life; being thankful.

Gratefulness Stuffing spreads kindness and appreciation to others. In a world filled with materialism, it seems that gratefulness has gone out the window. If you speak to generations who had limited material things, you will find they appreciate what they have, without a need to get more, and emphasize relationships over things.

People from this era gathered more often, worked together — and were hands on for the advantage of all. In that day, there were no distractions, such as cell phones or computers.

I largely believe that gratefulness is a learned behavior and is acquired through the progression of life and maturity. Watching a *Piñata Role Model,* who focuses their actions and words on kindness and love, is a natural way to load the *Gratefulness Stuffing.*

It is very important to include gratefulness into your day. Buy a note book and write down all of the things you are grateful for. Some people say there is nothing to be grateful for. This is not true. There is always something to be grateful for if we look.

We can easily focus on negative things that happen to us in life. These disappointments can knock the stuffing out of our Piñata, leading to sadness, depression, hopelessness, and feelings of failure. Negative experiences happen. Heal yourself and move forward. Don't steal your own joy today, for things that cannot be changed. Don't borrow trouble worrying about things that probably will never happen.

When we shift our mind to focus on gratefulness, we will acknowledge how many things in our life are absolute blessings.

Think Outside of Your Piñata

When you experience a seemingly unexplainable event in your life — accept these moments as they truly are — a blessing. We often discard such incidents, referring to them as being *weird* or *a coincidence*. Stop what you are doing and say thank you to the heavens.

I literally say, "Thank You, God," when something happens that I know He did for me. I raise my hands to the sky and look up while I verbally communicate this. I don't care who I am with or where I am, I do it.

The gratefulness connection comes from the conscious mind and the spirit. A grateful mind has no room for self-pity, jealousy, anger, self-abuse and other things that can trap us in a state of despair.

Gratefulness needs to be humble, meaning, focused on the basic needs of human survival — food, shelter, water, sunshine, and clothing. I pray often, thanking God for these gifts in my life. What we may take for granted is a huge blessing to millions of people around the world who do without.

Gratefulness extends to the people we have in our life by appreciating how much of a blessing they are. Regardless of different opinions and slight annoyances that can pull us from the beauty of relationship, when we look, we can see positive potential.

I thank people often — from the grocery store clerks to the local garage. I thank people for what they do in regard to their work, and praise them for a job well done or exceptional service.

Gratefulness is being thankful just because we are alive and healthy. I watch and hear about all of the horrible wars around the world, repressed people, poverty and terrorism and quickly realize how truly blessed I am. If we spent one day in these people's shoes we would quickly realize how fortunate we truly are.

After going to third world countries, my heart is heavy. I thank God for what I have been given and I pray for blessings upon them. If you are blessed with money and good fortune, pass this blessing to others to help them survive, learn and thrive.

Gratefulness spreads goodwill and kindness to others. Gratefulness removes unnecessary stuff from our home and gives these things to others in need.

Gratefulness involves a meaningful appreciation for life and the natural beauty that surrounds us: air, water, trees, sunshine, flowers, animals, stars, the feeling of the wind in our face, the twinkle of sunlight on the water and running through the grass barefoot.

Gratefulness leads us away from needing and buying things to being fulfilled. Life itself, having basic needs, living our purpose, and praising God, all keep us joyful. Gratitude is necessary to our survival, and as we'll discover next, often comes from surprising situations.

Chapter Thirty-Four
Signs-From-Heaven Stuffing

In one week, I went to three funerals of women who were in the prime of life and died of cancer. All of these women were between the ages of forty-six to fifty-seven years.

Prior to attending the first visitation, I was reading a few pages from a book Stacey gave me called *You Can You Will*, by *Joel Osteen* — an incredible minister and author. My colorful 3D *butterfly* bookmark was placed in the book. I opened the book at this spot and Joel wrote about God leading us to do the things we were destined to do, such as *writing a book*. I had been saying for years that I was going to *write a book one day*.

On the way to the funeral, I was listening to an inspirational radio program out of Detroit, Michigan. The pastor was talking about each of us having special gifts and sometimes it takes another person to help us see the gifts we have. The other person *unwraps* or *opens us up* to see what's inside. Hmmm, makes me think of opening a Piñata to see what's inside! The pastor continued to say that we may not see what talents we have, such as *writing a book*. Gulp.

I arrived at the visitation and there was heavy sadness at the passing of this young woman — a wife, sister, daughter, friend and mother of four young children. Brenda was a writer and wrote many poems and also had an inspirational website. Her books were spread throughout the funeral home on tables. One particularly caught my eye as it was surrounded by *butterflies*. Through her cancer treatments, Brenda shared her poems with others in treatment, to encourage them in their journey.

I can remember her brother, John, telling me that Brenda was never a writer, which surprised me. She attended a CORE weekend, which is a spiritual retreat, and from there she began writing as though something was writing through her. Everything flowed through Brenda onto paper — her poems were beautiful and so meaningful.

Driving home after the visitation, I thought of Brenda's family and loved ones — how devastating her passing was to all of them. I also thought about the butterflies that surrounded her books and poems. The butterfly is my animal spirit guide, representing change and transformation. I knew years ago that the butterfly was speaking to me, reminding me to spread my wings and fly and to move forward regardless of the weight on my wings. Brenda changed in form, from physical and spirit, to pure spirit transforming to another dimension — heaven.

When I arrived home, I shared the heavy-hearted experience of Brenda's funeral with my daughter, Lisa, and her fiancé, Sebastian. As I sat beside them on the couch, I texted Stacey about Brenda's funeral as well. I also told him about the universe's triple knock, knock, knock that was guiding me to write a book.

Lisa, (not knowing what I was texting) said impatiently, "Mom, what are you doing! Writing a book?" referring to my lengthy texts to Stacey. The universe provided yet another "*sign*" and it was crystal clear: I needed to write a book, before *my time* was up!

This very week as I write this, Stacey's sister passed and I experienced a Native funeral for the first time. I looked at her body, resting in the coffin in her home as guests were milling around, praying, singing, drumming, crying, or reflecting. I looked at her tiny face and it showed the years of hardship and her final battle with cancer. A colorful large feather was placed gently behind her head and it peaked out above her black hair.

Time stands still when you see a person's lifeless body in a coffin. Life's frailty becomes incredibly profound — one day it will cease for all of us. It is a guaranteed final curtain call, one-way ticket, with no return. Our Piñata's shell will lie in a grave or be minimized to dust in an urn. The spirit within us leaves and transcends into the spiritual realm. I knew Colleen already left days ago to another world. I felt happy she had left this planet and went to a much better place.

My family doctor Avril passed the same week. The woman, who dedicated her life to medicine and helping thousands of patients, lost her life to cancer. It was surreal to see the one who healed many, die. There were hundreds of people who passed through the visitation.

At Avril's funeral, I walked alongside a lady named Jeannie, and we introduced ourselves to each other. We ended up chatting for the next two hours as we shuffled closer to the reception line. We reminisced about Avril and shared a bit about each other.

Avril really helped me when I went through my mental crash. I can remember walking into her office and *she* started to cry. Avril knew that what had happened was not me. She was very helpful at that time, and her genuine concern for me was authentic. I was grateful for her care and also for her healing hand with my children — she delivered Jordan into the world. She always had a beautiful smile.

As Jeannie and I moved closer and closer, I looked down at Avril's memorial card that I picked up on the way in. There was another card that was distributed, with a picture of praying hands on one side. As I looked at the praying hands, I said to Jeannie that the other side most certainly must have the poem *Footprints* written on it. I flipped the card to the other side and it was *blank*. Jeannine looked at her card and it had the *Footprints* poem written on it.

"That's odd", Jeannie said looking puzzled, referring to my card being blank.

I said, "No, there is always a reason for everything."

I knew mine was blank, as heaven was telling me I needed to write, in order to fill the empty space. I also needed to pray. This card sits on a night stand in my bedroom and I look at it every night. It reminds me of Avril and prayer.

The heavens spoke to me at each funeral wake. I thanked God for these beautiful women and the blessings they gave to others who loved them. I heard many stories about how each of them touched countless lives. Each walked a completely different path, yet they were all very loving and believed in God. They had a willingness, desire and purpose to help others. They left a wonderful legacy. What will you leave?

My dear Piñatas, what is your legacy going to be, during your time on earth?

How will you love? How will you serve? What part of your stuffing will you share, to heal, bless and inspire others? If your stuffing's in a pinch, don't fret, get your Piñata hooves moving to the ground and start working on yourself. We learn every single day — enriching our mind, body and spirit as a result. Life is a journey. We did not come equipped with a How-to-Guide-for-Piñatas at birth, so accept your faults and rejoice in your inherent ability to evolve and Step into Piñata Greatness.

Chapter Thirty-Five
How to Have Your Best Life – Regardless of Your Past Stuffing!

Human Piñatas have the tremendous ability to heal, change, grow and achieve, regardless of their past.

But some of you might have deeply buried secrets you have not shared with other Piñatas because you may feel responsibility, shame, fear, or guilt. Each of us has had different life experiences and no two Piñatas are the same. Yet we are similar in that every Piñata has experienced pain, regret and made mistakes. No one feels good about that, but this is all part of being HUMAN. We make mistakes and do things we wish we would have done differently. The best way to get past your stuffing is to get counseling in areas you feel you have not had closure, understanding, or healing about. Maybe you haven't even spoken it to anyone else.

When we hurt others or do something wrong, it is very important to apologize to the person we hurt or victimized. It takes a brave Piñata to admit to being wrong, hurtful or abusive toward another Piñata. We must swallow our pride and ego stuffing and admit our faults.

To move on from past negative experiences, the key lies in accepting the impossibility of changing events from the past. Even if we wish we could. All we can do is evolve forward — through honest reflection of self, by recognizing the valuable lesson and healing through forgiveness.

I suggest that you create a *Piñata Top 10 — Life Lessons List*. Write down the top life lessons you learned each year in a journal. Be honest and insightful. As you move forward in life, review and acknowledge the great progress and discoveries you have made. Celebrate your victories, lessons, awareness and growth. Your top life lessons should include recognizing your achievements and personal transformation, such as a new lifestyle, learned skills, and Piñata Ah-Ha Moments.

If I have done something I am ashamed of or feel I have hurt someone, I apologize to the person I affected. I follow with a prayer asking God for forgiveness for what I did. I speak to God and tell him how sorry I am for my actions. I know and believe that God forgives you and I. He does not want us to dwell on the sorrow again. Once it is forgiven, you must move forward with what you have learned in the situation and use this knowledge to benefit you and others in the future.

The Heavy-Piñata-Wagon with Piñata Poop

Please don't pull guilt, shame, blame, and remorse stuffing around with you. It's like pulling a wagon of *Piñata Poop*, everywhere you go. This is stinky business, and the weight of it pulls your Piñata down.

Stop for a moment and visualize yourself pulling a wagon behind you, (*The Heavy-Pinata-Wagon*) every step of *your life*. Go to church, work, or to a family reunion and bring that wagon of negative stuffing with you. How do you feel when you picture this?

This wagon filled with *Piñata Poop* is going to hold you back, not to mention, your arm will get sore and your heart will feel heavy. You may think no one can see your wagon, but they do. They will say, (under their breath), "Is he still pulling that poop around? It's been five years. When is he going to *let it go*?"

Forgiveness is the Key to Freedom!

Forgiveness is the key to freedom from emotional bondage. When we hold hate and anger toward others, that mindset keeps us trapped in a space that limits us from experiencing the fullness of life.

For years, I carried around anger towards people who had hurt me. All I was really doing was telling my body, mind, spirit and every cell, *I am angry.* Instead of focusing on what I could change today, I dwelled on the past — already engraved in stone.

We cannot control the actions of others, but we can choose to stop pulling them around in a wagon with us everywhere we go. Here I go with the *Piñata Poop* again. Did this make you giggle? From your Piñata toes?

Put the person who hurt you in the same wagon, on top of the Piñata Poop — make that load super heavy, after all, it's your *entire load to bare.* Does this picture seem silly, yet helpful?

Use my *Heavy-Piñata-Wagon* example, when you begin to think of a person who hurt you. See them sitting in a wagon full of Piñata Poop, following you everywhere. Stop smiling, this is serious.

Now watch as you drop the wagon handle and walk away. Do you feel lighter? Free? Released of physical and emotional pain? You should!

Chapter Thirty-Six
The Shock of My Life

In the fall of 2016, I became ill. I underwent several tests trying to diagnose my symptoms. I took time off work and was experiencing lightheadedness, a severe rash, exhaustion and my fibromyalgia was flared to the point that I needed to grab a handrail to go down my steps in the morning.

Stacey was having financial issues for a few months and was deep into a family dispute regarding an estate. He used my car for a few months as a result. Stacey would come to my house more often, as I was ill, versus me going to his house.

My enabling started a while back in this relationship. Stacey lived on the edge of poverty, so I'd pull my wallet out most of the time. He often went away for pow-wows, training and taking people to rehab. His volunteer work schedule increased to the point that it was affecting our relationship.

Stacey always had excuses for why his bingo shifts were doubling. He would be late, or cancel us getting together, as something happened to someone in the community, tying him up. I'd justify this, thinking he was a good man, as he was always giving, helping and volunteering.

I noticed that he was spending less and less time with his daughter. I questioned this, and he said due to her age, she was more interested in her friends. His daughter lived on a nearby reserve with her mother. The issues continued with the estate of his sister, so his vehicle was in limbo. Finally, I said enough was enough, I needed my car back.

I was getting annoyed with one excuse after another. He was so cute and smiled from ear to ear, so he was hard to get pissed off at. He returned my car and I attended a local car dealer to look at vehicles with him. He was going to buy a used vehicle and forfeit his vehicle, as the estate issue was still unsettled. I had no idea how he would manage two payments, but that wasn't my issue. Stacey needed to accept responsibility.

The dealer did a background check and found that he owed a substantial amount of money on his old beat up SUV (the one being held under the estate of his sister), likely 10x the actual price of what he could get for it. His SUV was a pile of junk, with over 350,000km, it even had tape to hold up the window. We'd often use my vehicle, especially to go to family events. I truthfully felt ashamed of his vehicle — my family would have been very concerned had they seen how he managed his wheels.

The salesperson pointed out all of his financial problems and that a creditor would loan him money for the vehicle he was looking at for a very high rate of interest and money down. I sat there and thought, *I am NOT co-signing. He got himself in this pickle.*

Stacey then told the salesperson that his financial situation was going to improve. I looked over at him as he told the salesperson that he was likely moving in with his brother Dave. I just about fell off my chair, while my blood pressure soared.

I sat quietly as they filled out the paperwork. Stacey then told the salesman that he was getting a raise at work — yet another important life moment that he should have shared with me, but didn't. A complete stranger knew more about my boyfriend than I did, in ten minutes. Stacey and I discussed everything openly and getting a raise would have been something to celebrate.

We left the car dealer and the silence could cut the air. Stacey and

I talked that day and many times about our future. He always told me, "Don't worry baby, we are together, we are committed." He asked me what was wrong as I drove away. I told him that the salesperson knew more about him than I did.

We stopped at the grocery store and he tagged along like a puppy fresh in trouble. I was furious and said nothing.

I finally looked at him and said, "When were you going to tell me you were moving in with your brother?"

Stacey said that it was not a for sure thing and that he had talked to some of his sisters about his brother's situation. There were issues at his brother Dave's house. The brother was in a wheelchair since his early teens and was now in his forties.

Drug users were in and out of the house and the police recently attended there. Stacey told me a few weeks prior that the police were at Dave's house because of a situation. Stacey said that the police arrived to find drugs and a man naked in a bedroom masturbating on an air mattress while looking at porn. Dave was smoking pot and let these people in.

Stacey said that one or more of his sisters suggested someone needed to be with Dave, to live with him, to police him. Since Stacey was single and not married, he should babysit Dave.

I said, "Really? What if you and I were married with two kids and Dave was misbehaving, would you get up and leave?"

I added, "Dave lets these people in his house. He's a grown man."

I suggested that it would be cheaper to buy a camera and a monitor. I asked why other members of the family weren't stepping up and policing Dave. One sister literally lives on the same lot, right next door.

Stacey was silent in the grocery store. He knew I was not a happy Piñata.

I looked at him and a complete thought dropped down from

nowhere and right out of my mouth, "Is there someone else?"

"Of course not, *baby (one of his pet words for me)*. I barely have time for you, me or anything, let alone another person," he responded.

This was true. Stacey was the excessive volunteer. He was constantly overdoing everything. If anyone died on the Island, he was asked to help at the funeral. There seemed to be a rash of deaths, for a very small community.

When we got home, I cried as I prepared our dinner. Something was off. Stacey did not respond, sitting in silence. This was unusual for him. He never acted this way. We never fought.

I asked him why he wasn't sensitive to my feelings. Stacey finally got up off his seat when I asked him why he was acting in such an uncaring manner. When I questioned him about the status of our relationship, and our goal of being together, he agreed that that he would move in with me next summer.

I was relieved, seeing a glimpse of Stacey again. Two years together was developing into a permanent plan. We never fought, we communicated, we laughed, we had a great sex life, everyone liked him, including my children. I believed we were both content. I trusted him.

Many Friday nights, I would sit home while he volunteered at the Bingo. He was the President of the Walpole Island Community Bingo Association. His shifts became more and more.

But an odd thing began to happen to me on nights I was home alone, while Stacey was at Bingo. A thought dropped into my mind, out of no-where. I vividly saw him lying in bed *naked with a woman.* I pictured myself walking into his house to visit and seeing them tangled up in the bed. *Where were these images and thoughts coming from?*

I'd shake my head and think, *Charlene, how could you think those thoughts? Stacey loves you. He's always doing good for others.*

Besides, Stacey always sent me pictures of him smiling, showing me what he was doing. Pictures included him bringing his disabled brother shopping, time with his daughter, his pow-wow excursions, his training out of town and even him smiling cooking at the bingo. I thought, *What an angel Stacey is — my angel!*

Some nights I would text him with no response. I'd worry all night.

The next day he'd finally respond, make like it was no big deal, and say I shouldn't worry, because after all, "I am a grown man." He said he was in an area with poor cell phone reception which was common on the island. And, I believed him.

Lisa and Sebastian were home from Germany in 2016 and several guests attended to visit them at my home. Stacey helped with everything. I was limited to what I could do because of my illness, so he stepped up by cooking, cleaning, setting up and doing a lot of work. I was very grateful.

All the women at the BBQ sat in awe of Stacey and gushed over how sweet he was, watching him set up the food and later clean everything up.

They said, "Wow, he's super."

I said, "Yes, I am so lucky."

Stacey just ate that up and smiled. He kissed me in front of them.

I had not gone to Stacey's home in a very long time because of my illness. He was more than happy to drive to my place so that we could be together.

A month later, Stacey and I were approaching our second anniversary, his birthday and Thanksgiving. We had much to celebrate.

I made a beautiful dinner for our anniversary and Stacey came in with beautiful roses. We greeted each other with our usual big kiss, tight hug and smiles. I took pictures and posted these beautiful life moments on *Facebook*. We got lots of high fives and support.

My family and friends were happy that I had finally found a mate who appeared to be a fit. Regardless of his lack of material things, he was rich in spirit. He was always positive.

After our anniversary, his birthday, and our families' Thanksgiving, we departed. Before leaving Walpole Island, after celebrating Thanksgiving with his sister's family, I suggested that I could stay overnight at his place. He said he was going to try and get together with his daughter. Before that, he said he needed to stop by his brother's house. It was on the same lot as his sister's home, the one we'd just left. We kissed, hugged and smiled. I drove away and headed home.

When I was nearly back to my place, a text message popped up on my phone. I pulled over and saw that it was a friend of mine. She wrote "I am not sure how to ask this. Are you and Stacey in an open relationship?"

Gulp.

I was confused. I was frazzled. I wrote, "What do you mean?" thinking I was reading her message incorrectly.

I continued texting, "No, we are not."

She wrote, "I don't know how to tell you this. Stacey is on a dating site and sent me a message a few days ago."

My heart sank. I was in shock.

My friend sent me a picture of his dating profile. His name was different. He was single. His picture was one I had seen on his *LinkedIn* account recently.

He was looking for friendship, to see where it may lead.

As I type these words and relive the scenario in my mind, my heart is pounding, reliving this. It is very painful.

I called Stacey. No answer. I left a message for him to call me, and said it was urgent. There must be a reasonable explanation. I justified to myself, *My angel would never be on a dating site. He loves me.*

I sent another text for him to call me ASAP. Again, I said it was urgent.

He called, "What's the matter baby, is everything okay? Is your family okay?"

I asked him where he was, to which he responded, that he was in the community just outside of the reserve. I thought, *Gee, you said you were driving out of town to the next reserve to see your daughter, which is forty minutes away. Why was he in town?*

So, I said, meet me at the local coffee shop. Ten minutes passed, everything seemed so surreal. My heart was pounding. Finally, at the coffee shop, I pulled in beside his vehicle.

Stacey immediately got out of his car and into mine.

He said, "Baby, what's the matter, is everything okay?"

Barely able to breathe due to anxiety, I said, "You tell me."

He asked, "What do you mean?"

I said, "Tell me."

He stared at me in silence, just as he did in the grocery store. I said my friend sent me a message showing me his profile on a dating site and I showed the snapshot of his profile. He said that the profile was old.

I said, "Gee, funny the picture on your profile is recent, since we have been dating." He stared.

I then told him that my friend received a message from him. Dead silence. I told him it was time to tell the truth.

He blurted, "I don't want to be committed."

I replied with, "How many women have you slept with?"

He said, "None."

I looked at him, still in shock. The unfolding details were slicing through my heart with a dagger. It was a nightmare.

I said, "Do you have my house keys?"

I had given him keys to my home to watch it while I was away at my daughter's wedding in Germany, earlier that summer. While I was gone, he sent me pictures of all the things he did around the yard, and him lying in my bed, with his head on my pillow, eating a piece of red *Twizzlers* licorice, smiling.

I always found it odd that he would leave candy in my lingerie drawer. But, I just thought, *Oh, how sweet is he.*

Now I think this is one of his ways of leaving his mark, when he struck gold. I wonder, *how many women had candy from him, left in their dressers?*

He pulled my keys out, and I said, "Give them to me. We are finished."

Boom, it was done. The beautiful face, personality, smile, person, my love, was gone.

He slithered to his vehicle. I got out of my car and said, "Is that it? Two years and that's all you can say?"

Stacey's face was like stone, he muttered that he didn't want to take care of me. His sister died, his mother died — because they were sick.

He said he could not handle another death. I was not dying. I think he had to say something, anything, even if totally unrealistic, to justify his actions.

I went home still reeling from the shocking news. I went into the house, feeling destroyed. I posted Stacey's dating profile on my Facebook, and wrote, "After two years, our anniversary, his birthday and family Thanksgivings, I found out tonight Stacey has been on a dating site." Facebook lit up like a Christmas tree.

I knew I needed to post the truth. People were in shock, as they would have never expected him to be this way. Just four days before, I had posted pictures of us celebrating special moments including his smiling face holding a beautiful bouquet of flowers, at which time I wrote, "Two years and going strong."

Everything was gone in an instant.

The very next day, I returned to work after being sick for weeks. Referring back to my sickness, the doctors concluded that it was fibromyalgia, depression and anxiety. I also had issues with my arm/shoulder that was being tended to.

I walked in and my co-workers were quite silent. I got a few hugs. Some had seen my post the night before. Another revelation came from a co-worker. He knew that Stacey had been on dating sites months before — at least six months.

Stacey had also contacted a woman in the building I worked in. He even tried to get her attention as she walked down the hall, moments after he talked to me and gave me a hug. That same day, I introduced him to co-workers who had never met him. Embarrassing now, beyond comprehension, how he played me like a fiddle.

I was upset that my co-worker didn't tell me this. He said he wanted to, but I was always speaking highly of Stacey. I returned a response to him, indicating that months of not knowing that he was cheating, may result in health issues for me, if Stacey contracted STD's from another female. We did not use protection. He made like he was single for a long time before he met me, not focused on women at all, and was in one long term relationship.

Stacey owed me a few hundred dollars and left it in an envelope in my mailbox overnight. No note, nothing. The horror flared in me again. I texted him saying how could he have done this to us? He said he was sorry for hurting me and my family and that he didn't want commitment. Never told me that. Not once.

I ended up speaking with a counselor at the EAP program which my employer offers to help us through difficult life moments. He felt that I deserved more than a five-minute conversation with Stacey, in order to have closure. I texted Stacey asking to talk and I received no response. That week, after work I drove to the reserve. My heart pounded. I kept telling myself to remain calm.

I drove to his house and there were unfamiliar vehicles in his driveway. I walked up, my heart pounding. A man opened the door. I saw more people inside.

The man said, "Yes?"

I said, "Where is Stacey?"

He replied, "He *moved out months ago.*"

The lies got deeper and deeper. I drove to the main road on the Reserve and spotted his vehicle in the driveway, at the same location where I had Thanksgiving at his sisters, five days before.

There were three houses on this lot. His sister's, his brother Dave's (the place he said he had to stop at after our dinner on Thanksgiving) and his deceased mothers home, abandoned for some time.

His vehicle was parked at his mother's old house. I went to the door and knocked. Stacey answered the door, his face blank. I asked if we could talk and he let me in. The love I knew was gone. He would not respond to me; his stare was dark and he stood emotionless.

Do you recall how I described him as being very spiritual, kind, loving and grateful? It was as though he had a split personality and I was just meeting his other half.

All of his belongings were piled up everywhere. He was installing shelves — those that I gave to him to organize the previous house he was living at. The same house that we started our relationship in.

I asked him to tell me the truth, including how many people he had seen and slept with. He said three. My heart dropped into my gut. I said, "How could you do this, *to us?*"

I asked him who *his God* was. He always spoke of Creator, love, gratefulness, and portrayed a spirit like no other person I had ever met. He said nothing.

I said, "My God is about love and truth. You are still an addict, using sex instead of drugs to fill your void."

He said nothing.

I told him that when I die and stand before God, I will be proud of the way I treated him — with complete love.

"Stacey, what are you going to say to God? I thought *you* were the Phoenix who rose above the ashes. YOU were the one that beat the odds!" I was referring to his life transition from an abusive childhood, drugs and crime, to becoming a light on the Reserve. He was a master at smoke and mirrors.

Stacey came from a very difficult childhood. Both of his parents attended residential schools. They were damaged. There was violence, drug abuse and constant chaos. The house was literally a bar. Stacey said that his mom and dad would beat each other.

Drunks would be passed out on the floor and the young children would roll them.

I said, "What does that mean, roll them?"

He said when the drunks passed out, they would roll them over and take their wallet and money.

The Children's Aid Society had removed the eleven children on and off, including Stacey and one of his sisters who ended up in a foster home together for a couple years. I met his foster Mom and Dad at the community pow-wow that Stacey organized the last summer we were together.

The foster mom said they wanted to permanently adopt Stacey and his sister. They were devastated to learn that they were going back to their natural parents. Tears filled her eyes.

Stacey's family was no stranger to the criminal justice system. Stacey was in and out of jail in his teens and early twenties. He also abused drugs and alcohol at this time.

We met when he was forty-six years old. I always asked him how he managed to escape all of this past and become the person he had become. He said he knew that it was not right and not in line with what he was created to be. God had wanted more for him.

I stood in the room looking at Stacey. I tried to hug him and also to kiss him. He was like a corpse. I don't know why I did that, maybe thinking there was still something there. There wasn't. He was cold and lifeless.

The house was completely in ruins. There was a two-inch crack in the wall, where the rays of daylight beamed through. The floors were totally worn, one area I could see the dirt of the ground beneath. Why would Stacey want this? It was a dump. It should have been bull-dozed. He was fixing it up to live in. He had little money. This wasn't realistic. He was avoiding reality.

I told him that he still had a criminal mind. He cheated, lied, deceived and stole people's goodwill. One of his brothers came by (an older brother that he seldom spoke about) and Stacey showed him what he needed to do to fix it up. Stacey was in complete denial of what was evident in front of his eyes. A great example of existing and thinking in *Piñata La-Land Land*.

I said, "Hello, I'm Charlene. Stacey and I have been dating for two years and he was going to move in with me, yet wants to live here," in a sarcastic tone.

No response. I put my hand on Stacey's, trying to hold it like we always did, yet it was lifeless.

The guy I fell in love with was gone. The entity that stood in front of me was not him. Everything about him was unrecognizable. On our anniversary, I wrote a beautiful letter. I remember him opening it and reading it. I talked about our amazing love, our journey, wonderful memories and how proud I was of him for being such a spiritual person who was a positive example and leader in his community.

After he read it, he said, "Thank you, baby." We were happy and our relationship was wonderful, so I thought.

Stacey said to me that he didn't want commitment. One sentence, that's it. He admitted to sleeping with three women. I asked him how it felt, having sex with me and having sex with others. I asked him if he told them he loved them, how beautiful they were and if he looked into their eyes as we did.

The dark entity stared at me, nothing.

I asked him if he did things to them that he did to me. We used to howl like wolves, laughing after sex. He'd tell me how much he loved me and vice versa.

Stacey said that the sex he had with them was *consensual*, like that mattered to me and had anything to do with his cheating.

It was yet another misaligned justification for his actions. The women agreed, so what is wrong with what he did? It wasn't like he raped them or pushed sex on them. Stacey's *Bullshit-Stuffing* was in full throttle.

The only thing that slipped his mind is that he didn't mention it to me or ask me if it was okay for him to have sex with several women while with me! He lied over and over, telling me he was busy, yet he was rolling naked with other women.

Gulp. Big sigh.

That was it. The last time we spoke.

I walked away, got in my car and pulled up to the roadway, numb from head to toe at what I had just seen. I stopped and a thought dropped down....my mother's quilt! I reversed the car and went to the door.

I knocked and he opened the door. I said, "Where's my mother's quilt? I want it back. You do not deserve it."

My mother gave him a handmade quilt. I remember when I gave it to him. He smiled and was appeared so happy. He wrapped it around him while standing up. I snapped a picture from my phone and sent it to Mom. He smiled from ear to ear. His smile was beautiful. He could have been a model. His jet-black thick hair framed his chiseled cheek bones and dark brown eyes. His skin was like a perfect tan. I often joked with him, that I wished I was Native, just to have that skin.

Stacey gave me the quilt. No exchange of words. I turned around, tears in my eyes and left. My family often donated things to the community through Stacey. There was extreme poverty. When his sister died, some of my family came to support him.

After the fall-out, the truth reared its ugly head in the days to come. I found out that Stacey had sent lingerie to a woman he didn't even date. Stacey also used *LinkedIn* to pick up women, using his spiritual words to lure them in. His profile was that of a very caring person, full of love and gratefulness.

We met on *LinkedIn*. He lured me in like a predator using candy to groom vulnerable children. He did not have the reputation that he created for me. He was not respected. He had an ugly truth that he hid from me, including a distorted sexual past. His past was much more extensive than he admitted to.

Many nights, I'd lie in bed and reach over to where he used to sleep. I couldn't cross the invisible line to go on *that side* of the bed. I dared not touch the pillow he laid his head on because it now felt dirty. Everything in this bed felt dirty. I threw out the pillows and washed the sheets over and over, getting rid of all the lies.

My co-workers, family and friends still reeled over the illusion in disbelief. I had many calls and visits, encouraging me, loving me and helping me get through the shock. I thank two very wonderful people — Rosa and Carlos, for reaching out at this very difficult time and sharing things that helped me believe in me.

My friends and co-authors in *The Change* book series also reached out to me.

One in particular gave me very insightful thoughts to reflect upon.

Sally said that Stacey likely felt that he'd never live up to my world. He loved me, but his scars were too deep. Stacey was unable to escape his past, regardless of his efforts to escape. It pulled him right back in, with no mercy. His subconscious stuffing was so powerful, his conscious efforts to change were no match.

Stacey also went on dating sites while with a woman he was in a common law relationship for years. They had a child together. He said he left her because *she cheated on him.* I found out that he was cheating on her and she eventually found someone to bond to. Again, justification for his actions, blaming someone else, not taking responsibility.

She said that Stacey would never have a healthy relationship until he dealt with the events in his past, from his childhood — that he never healed or got counseling for *it.* She didn't come right out and say what *it* was, but I know it was sexual. He had a sick sense of what commitment was. She also said, "How can a man with so many great qualities, have such a dark side." I agreed.

I highly sense that he was likely sexually abused. He was still stuck in the stuffing of his past. I don't even know if one word out of his mouth was the truth. I will never know the extent of any of it. One of his brothers later told me that Stacey was broken and never got help.

I later found out that he carried on a relationship with a woman in another city, for the majority of the time that we dated. She never knew he was in a relationship. He lied to her too. She said she was sorry and very sickened, as was I. She had never seen this in him. It wasn't her fault, I told her.

Her intuition wondered about some things, but she would always believe him. Like me, she put her inner voice aside, instead of asking/ investigating more about him.

Another Hard Lesson & Forgiveness

Another life lesson hurled at me — this time about acceptance, self-awareness, healing and forgiveness.

After the death of our relationship, I went through all of the grieving stages: shock, denial, anger, then finally acceptance. I decided that I would transition through each stage and fight the convenience of becoming trapped within the battle inside my head — the dirt from my subconscious mind.

It was not simple to change old patterns of self-defeat. I stopped the bubbles of stuffing that floated to the forefront of my thoughts. This old stuffing convinced me that *all men are jerks* and, *I'm not pretty or lovable enough* to have stopped Stacey from cheating on me. *I wasn't enough*. I surely must have been totally stupid not to have seen this coming. I trusted.

These thoughts were not truthful nor serving anyone. I stopped every thought that surfaced, like a child holding a plastic hammer whacking the head of pop up figures in succession, playing a game at the fair.

I decided to forgive him. I prayed for him, to get help and to find peace. I prayed for compassion and understanding. I cannot imagine what he went through as a child. It must have been horrifying at times.

As much as he loved his family, there was an apparent, huge separation and discord between many. He did not have similar relationships as I did with my family. Stacey seemed to enjoy my family, often greeting, talking and hugging them. As a child, he seen and experienced events, not by choice, but by birth — with no escape.

Interesting that after the breakup, my fibromyalgia improved to a point of my body feeling normal again. I believe that my spirit was totally aware of the truth and attempted to shut my physical body down (again) to wake me up. Spirit is always aware of the truth.

When you get a gut feeling or a knowing, that's your spirit. It is speaking. Listen dear Piñata, listen! When we don't listen to our inner voice, we will experience pain over and over until we get it.

My conscious mind ultimately chose to move forward, knowing I could not change others, only myself. How I chose to handle this, would either dishonor my spirit through hate, anger and resentment or glorify its sacred existence through love.

Pain is inevitable in life, suffering is not. We choose whether we want to pull a wagon full of shit around with us every day. We choose if we want to live in the love, support and truth of God.

Chapter Thirty-Seven
A Grand Plan Unfolding

In 2017, I was contacted by Steven, a gentleman who survived the residential school system. Ironically, he found me on *LinkedIn*. Scary, but true. Steven was born in Stanley Mission, a First Nation settlement in northern Saskatchewan and eventually migrated to another reserve in northern Ontario, Canada. Steven asked me to join a team of people, to guide the native people. He said he spoke with an elder, a seer, who told him to pray and the people he needed would come.

It is Steven's vision to help First Nation's people become healthy, to stop the cycle of victimization, end drug and sexual abuse, and see their people and communities flourish. I said I would help.

Steven said he understands how Stacey came to be, based on his past — influenced by his parents, who were survivors of residential school. Steven helped me heal from my lingering hurt. He opened my heart and mind to understand the reality of life for many native people, mostly the lasting impact of childhood trauma on their psyche and spirit.

Steven said that in many cases, the sick (unhealthy people) are leading the sick. He added that some of the biggest abusers are the ones in positions of authority. Steven claimed the native youth are committing suicide because of sexual abuse.

"It doesn't matter what reserve, he said, "it's rampant across Canada."

Steven's statement about sexual abuse on reserves, is true and becoming public. The Canadian Press posted a story on November 6, 2016, "Sexual abuse haunts children as open secret in indigenous communities."

Freda Enns, a woman who experienced sexual abuse growing up on a reserve, shared her story. When she was a baby, her mother sold her to a man for a bottle of beer. She was sexually molested by a number of men throughout her childhood.

The reporters wrote, "Child sexual abuse is a disturbing reality in many of Canada's First Nations, Metis and Inuit communities, research is beginning to show.

Extensive interviews with social scientists, indigenous leaders and victims undertaken over the past few months by The Canadian Press show that the prevalence of sexual abuse in some communities is shockingly high. And only now are prominent indigenous leaders speaking out publicly for the first time about the need for communities to take a hard look.

It's a painful legacy connected to almost 120 years of government-sponsored, church-run residential schools, where aboriginal leaders say many native children were physically and sexually molested by clergy and other staff.

The abused in turn became abusers, creating a cycle of childhood sexual violation that has spread in ever-expanding ripples from one generation to the next.

Within indigenous society, the knowledge that children are being molested is often an open secret -- but one to which few are willing to give voice. Instead, they dance around the words, talking instead about child welfare, bullying, substance abuse, intergenerational trauma and community conflict."

A subsequent news story in The Canadian Press, on Nov. 13, 2016, by the same reporters stated: "During a months-long investigation by The Canadian Press, a number of leading experts -- researchers, the head of Canada's national Inuit organization and former Truth and Reconciliation chairman Murray Sinclair -- have flagged alarming levels of sexual abuse in some indigenous communities and potential links to the aboriginal suicide crisis."

I said to Steven, "Where do we start?"

Steven and I know the challenges are steep. Steven has hand-selected a team and is seeking a First Nation Reserve that will welcome our approach and work collectively towards lasting, meaningful change. We bring our gifts of knowledge and experience, but more so, the desire to guide, teach and heal others through the *Holy Spirit*.

Steven and I trust *Creator* — (also known as *The Great Spirit* in Native American History) a powerful force that guides people in wisdom and survival. Creator will provide everything we need to succeed and thrive. He will open the hearts of the people, to receive words of wisdom, and ignite a fire within their spirit. The beauty of their inherent greatness, culture and connection to earth, will once again shine brightly.

My deepest desire is a world where every child and adult have a beautiful life.

Steven told me, "Charlene, you have a native spirit in a white body." I pondered his words. My spirit feels at home with native people. Was the vision I had in the sweat lodge, seeing myself native — dancing and celebrating, a prophetic glimpse of my past and my purpose here

Short & Sparkling Piñata Tip

All that you have experienced in your life, is teaching, testing and preparing you, to step into Piñata Greatness!

today?

Shifting from Physical to Spiritual

After my breakup with Stacey, the universe supported me in ways never imagined. Supportive people and unexpected opportunities appeared. I believe this happened, in part, because there was a shift in my mindset. I decided to keep my feet moving, choosing not to be debilitated by this situation.

I'm not saying it wasn't painful. I however remained focused on the message in the Serenity Prayer:

"God grant me the serenity
to accept the things I cannot change;
courage to change the things I can;
and wisdom to know the difference.

Living one day at a time;
enjoying one moment at a time;
accepting hardships as the pathway to peace;
taking, as He did, this sinful world
as it is, not as I would have it;
trusting that He will make all things right
if I surrender to His Will;
that I may be reasonably happy in this life
and supremely happy with Him
forever in the next.
Amen."

I prayed. A lot.

I prayed, asking God to help Stacey and all of the people who have been traumatized by others actions across this planet. I prayed for their deliverance and healing, and a life filled with joy, abundance and unlimited potential.

My life purpose also became clearer. I am here to be a humanitarian and teacher — helping others in their journey, here in the physical. I strive to guide them, to dwell beyond flesh and humanness, by living through their spirit.

I believe this is all a test, this life — to see if we escape our physical trappings and return to love.

How? Through your inner light – spirit.

Your spirit will guide you home, when you need to remember where you came from, and what your purpose is. We must abandon the battles of the mind, and return to the true source of peace, love and truth: God. The spirit is our built-in umbilical cord, connected directly to God.

When you walk in your daily life, be grateful for every second, every exchange, every moment, recognizing all of it, as a gift from God. Breathe it in into your lungs, down to your toes, all of it. Truly embrace and feel the energy within you and around you.

Step into Your Greatness – Share Your Gifts with The World

Now I ask you: What conscious choices can you make today to place your Piñata in a position of service, using your talents to bless others in this lifetime?

When you wake up and open your eyes — thank God for life, service and opportunity. Declare then and there, "I am going to do something wonderful today for myself, for people, for nature, and for animals, with the intention of serving God."

Stacey used to say, "A new day, a new joy." I hope that you return home to your truth — your spirit. It is there, it never left you. You have the ability to help many when you heal yourself.

Looking back, I now understand the significance of seeing a giant praying mantis in my childhood, and later, the pair that Stacey and I stumbled upon. The Greek word *mantis*, means prophet or seer. I believe these sightings were a sign of my life purpose — to guide others to live through Spirit, and to follow the will of God.

Further insights about life can be appreciated, by examining the brilliance of this mesmerizing creature. The praying mantis is named for its prominent front legs, which are bent and held together at an angle that suggests the position of prayer. Prayer is paramount to existence, as is oxygen. It is the miraculous foundation of communication and bonding with God.

The praying mantis is also known to be fruitful in her endeavors, through unwavering patience and stillness. Patience is the ability to accept or tolerate delays, problems, or suffering without becoming annoyed or anxious. Be patient and Trust in God. He promises eternal bliss in His kingdom. Be comforted knowing He is with you, through every storm. He will provide for His children.

The praying mantis displays stillness, teaching us to quiet the mind, to be still, and be one with your natural, instinctive state. It is in this place, we connect with Spirit and to God. All is possible here.

Psalm 46:10 (King James Bible) *"Be still, and know that I am God: I will be exalted among the heathen, I will be exalted in the earth."*

My time with Stacey and being in native communities, were preparing me for Steven's call. They are pieces of a puzzle, connecting together, revealing to me a glorious picture of my life purpose. I also see my puzzle piece contributing to the collective story of existence. What is your contribution to others and the greater good?

I am fully aware of my calling, to continue my spiritual journey towards enlightening self and others. I will be the ear and voice of the brokenhearted, the addicted and the lost, turning them inward, to their inner light. I believe that every Piñata craves and needs love and fellowship. Love and connection will save humanity, cure addiction, end wars, and dissolve hate, greed and poverty.

To me, the most precious element in life is to be led by *The Great Spirit* (or *The Holy Spirit*) to further our spiritual evolution, becoming what we were created to be — a mirror of God.

Piñatas, "Start a fire in your spiritual engine, the world is waiting for you to *Step into Greatness.*"

My Special Piñatas

A heartfelt thank you to my children Lisa and Jordan. You are the dearest part of my life. Spirit told me long ago that your innate gifts would bless many. Follow your inner guide. Remember these words, always: If you have faith, you have everything.

Thank you, Jerome, for all the things you do for Lisa, Jordan and I. Lilly too!

To my son-in-law Sebastian, from your Canadian Mom — welcome to the family. Thankyou Rose Marie and Josef for welcoming Lisa, Riley and Kato.

I am grateful for my parents Leo & Irene, and siblings: Diane (Roger), Corinne (Marc), James (Mona), Jerome (Karen), Joe (Brenda) and Dave. I love you all very much. You are a wonderful family of Piñatas, unique and special in so many ways.

Special thank you to Mom and Dad for caring for me in 2012. You stood by my side, loved me, and opened your home, to help me heal after a very difficult time. Because of you, I made it through. Few people are so fortunate to have parents who do what you do, for each of us. Through every storm and season of joy, you taught me love, perseverance and faith. I can still remember kneeling on our little prayer bench in the house, holding my hands perfectly, conversing with God. Congratulations on sixty five years of marriage!

I am equally grateful for the Paulin family who have loved and supported me for many years. Rheal was a super guy who was taken away from us, much too young. His cheerful personality shines through Lisa. I still smile when I think about his unique vocabulary of words, such as dibbermints = doberman pinscher.

I have the best nieces and nephews an Aunt could ever be blessed with: Jeremy, Adrian, Joel, Andre, Janelle, Pierre, Nicholas, Jonathan, Jay and Hollie. Your partners are equally loved and mirror the great people you are.

A huge thank you to Aunt Helen and Uncle Dennis Brown, who walked many mountains and valleys along my side. Your move to Chatham blessed my life. Thank you for always encouraging me to reach higher and to fulfill my destiny, including writing this book. You also engrained in me, to love myself, and how I deserved to be treated by others. Aunty Helen and Uncle D, you rock!

Dave and Todd, I am forever grateful for your love, leadership and mentorship towards Jordan. Your intervention was paramount in his health and recovery today. You are family.

Manny, you guided me out of the darkness and into the light. You burst open my subconscious mind and helped me acknowledge, and overcome, the painful stuffing in my Piñata. Thank you for pushing me to download new stuffing, adapt new behaviors and love myself.

Loads of appreciation to my amazing friends, who supported me and kept my inner light burning — Rosa & Carlos Corsini, Jonathan & Jeannie Glass, Bob & Stephanie Rose, Floyd Porter, Stephanie Hillman, Karaoke Bob Meloche, Moya Darling, Cheryl Bechard, Kari Viglasky, Sally Kay Miller, DeLano Collier (RIP), Deb Crow, Sharon Campbell-Rayment, Ed MacLean, John Collins, Marlene MacLennan and Dr. Rizwan Rafiq. To all who lighted my path, thank you.

To my co-workers and friends at "Base 4", you are my extended family. You are all very *Special* indeed. If the world could only see what we do every day to help humanity.

To my friends with the OPP Transport, you are the best!

Much gratitude to my professional associates and friends, at The Canadian Association of Professional Speakers (CAPS), Southwestern Ontario. You are individually deeply talented, passionate, and among the best speakers on the planet. As a group, we learn together, encourage one other, evolve our messaging and grow as experts.

Dan Martell — I often share your story of transformation with at-risk youth in my care. Kids need to be told that someone cares and believes in them. They have potential and their life has purpose. One word, one sentence, can, and does, change lives. Meeting you was a Godsend in perfect timing.

Tony Robbins UPW was amazing, life changing and came when I was heartbroken. Elena Schoenberger, "You Freaking Rock!" Thanks for holding me when every pain was released; screaming with me, jumping with me, dancing together and believing in me, as I believe in you. Firewalkers — we celebrated, pushed our fears away and unleashed our greatness together.

Anita Agers-Brooks, you sharpened my manuscript and challenged me to reach higher. Your honesty and professional editing skills, polished *The Piñata Theory™*. Thank you for your friendship and encouragement through this life-changing process.

Thank you to my friend Deb Crowe, a fellow co-author in *The Change* book series, for introducing me to Anita. Many amazing friendships and collaborations have grown from Jim Britt and Jim Lute's life-altering book series—*The Change*. I thank these innovative entrepreneurs for inviting me to be a co-author in 2016. Their coaching, leadership and mentoring have blessed many.

Carolyn Flower of Carolyn Flower International, your guidance from conception, to birthing *my baby* — *The Piñata Theory™,* was priceless. You are a publishing guru, an intuitive and an absolute pleasure to have as a consultant and friend.

For a list of my favorite books that have made an impact on my life, please go to www.charlenerenaud.com

Contact Information: info@charlenerenaud.com /
Tel: 519-436-3911 (Canada)

Sources of Information or Influence

Books:

➤ Dr. Carl Alasko, PhD. 2008. *Emotional Bullshit.* N.p.:Tarcher-Perigee

➤ Dr. Gabor Mate. 2008. *The Realm of Hungry Ghosts.* Toronto: Vintage Canada

➤ Joyce Meyer. 2002. *Battlefield of the Mind.* Tennessee: Faith-Words

➤ Robin Karse-Morse and Meredith S. Wiley. 2012. *The Sacred Sick: The Role of Childhood Trauma in Adult Disease.* New York: Basic Books

Wikipedia:

➤ *"Canadian Indian residential school system,"* Wikipedia, last modified January 22, 2018, https://en.wikipedia.org/w/index.php?title=Canadian_Indian_residential_school_system&oldid=821808911

➤ *"Grandma Moses,"* Wikipedia, last modified January 18, 2018, https://en.wikipedia.org/w/index.php?title=Grandma_Moses&oldid=821139940

➤ *"Ipperwash Crisis,"* Wikipedia, last modified January 16, 2018, https://en.wikipedia.org/w/index.php?title=Ipperwash_Crisis&oldid=820721635

➤ *"The Burning Bed,"* Wikipedia, last modified January 22, 2018, https://en.wikipedia.org/w/index.php?title=The_Burning_Bed&oldid=821740015

➤ *"The Serenity Prayer,"* Wikipedia, last modified January 11, 2018, https://en.wikipedia.org/w/index.php?title=Serenity_Prayer&oldid=819878182

News Sources:

➤ Heflik, Roman. *"A Holocaust Survivor's Path to Peace Forgiving Josef Mengele."* Spiegel Online, December 9, 2005, http://www.

spiegel.de/international/a-holocaust-survivor-s-path-to-peace-forgiving-josef-mengele-a-389491.html

➤ Kirkup, Kristy. *"Isolation a barrier to exposing sexual abuse in remote indigenous communities: Bellegarde."* The Canadian Press, Nov. 13, 2016, https://www.thestar.com/news/canada/2016/11/13/isolation-a-barrier-to-exposing-sexual-abuse-in-remote-indigenous-communities-bellegarde.html

➤ Kirkup, Kristy; Ubelacker, Sheryl. *"Open secret: Sexual abuse haunts children in indigenous communities."* The Canadian Press, November 6, 2016, https://www.thestar.com/news/canada/2016/11/06/open-secret-sexual-abuse-haunts-children-in-indigenous-communities.html

➤ Wood, John. *"Nine killed, 'including three kids,' as blaze rips through house on Ontario First Nation."* The Canadian Press, March 30, 2016, http://nationalpost.com/news/canada/pikangikum-house-fire-on-remote-first-nation-kills-nine

Film:

➤ Cazabon, Andrée, *"1ˢᵗ Nation Children Growing Up in 3ʳᵈ World Conditions."* Film. Executive Producer, Director, Writer: Andrée Cazabon, Cinematographer, Editor: Peter Shatalow. Kitchenuhmaykoosib Inninuwug, Ontario, Canada, 2010

Research Articles:

➤ Alexander, Dr. Bruce K. Study 1970. Published 1981. *"Addiction: The View from Rat Park, Study."* Simon Fraser University, British Columbia, Canada

Charlene's Professional Services & Product Line
www.charlenerenaud.com   info@charlenerenaud.com

The Piñata Theory™ Greeting Card Collection, based on the book,

The Piñata Theory ™ (2018)   *The Change*, Book 12 (2016)

Step into Piñata Greatness!
Professional Speaker, Author, Life Transformation Expert
Addiction, Mental Health, Coaching, Self-Awareness, Relationships

With Special Guest, Charlene Renaud - Life Coach, Speaker, Creator and Author of The Piñata Theory™

Invite your staff, club, or membership to a life-altering and spectacular day — *The Piñata Theory™ Official Piñata Party!*

Charlene will share delicious *Life-Changing Stuffing* from *The Piñata Theory™*, helping your fellow Piñatas:

- ✓ Experience Forgiveness and Healing
- ✓ Acquire Tolerance and Compassion
- ✓ Align with Your Authentic Self & Inner Voice
- ✓ Learn About the Damaging Effects of Racial Paradigms
- ✓ Discover the Beautiful Gems in Their Stuffing
- ✓ Annihilate Piñata Poop - Stuffing that Hurts Self & Others
- ✓ Step into Piñata Greatness — Rock Your Most Colorful Self

- ✓ Become Skilled in Piñata-Conscious-Over-Ride
- ✓ Learn Piñata Lingo to Smooth Your Day
- ✓ Locate & Download Transformational Stuffing
- ✓ The Power of Conscious Awareness - Building Resiliency
- ✓ Discovering the Piñata Code — Burst Through Your Shell

Rock your fellow Piñatas by hosting the world exclusive *Piñata Theory™ Official Piñata Party!* Groups of 50-100; 100-200; 200-500; 500-1000.

Guaranteed to be fun, expressive, colorful, sparkling and transformational. Charlene is going to knock the toxic stuffing out of you, (painlessly), and help you re-discover your playful, stress-free spirit and life purpose!

Dress your Personal Piñata comfortably — ready to dance, sing, cheer and celebrate!

Every Piñata who partakes is gifted with an autographed copy of *The Piñata Theory™* book.

Information & Booking: info@charlenerenaud.com

www.charlenerenaud.com

Charlene Renaud is a member of the Canadian Association of Professional Speakers, Global Speakers Federation and Certified Coaches Federation. As a professional speaker, she inspires others to *Step into Greatness*, through powerful keynotes, workshops and life coaching about self-awareness, healthy relationships, mental wellness, addiction and recovery, spiritual living, and life purpose.

Charlene is the creator of *The Piñata Theory*™, an original and powerful metaphor, about the long-lasting effect of life experiences, buried deep within the subconscious mind. Using the *Piñata* as a symbol, she discusses major influencers, belief systems and traumatic events, that leave people stuck, depressed, sick, limited, fearful, or bond by repetitive destructive behaviors. Through the gift of spirit, conscious focus, collective empowerment, truthfulness, love, purging of toxic stuffing, and downloading healthy stuffing, Charlene believes — all is possible. Charlene is also co-author in *The Change*, book 12, a global self-help series of books.

Charlene created the *Piñata Theory*™ *Greeting Card Collection* — a delightful group of Piñata characters, each depicting a special inspirational message on eight unique greeting cards. These cards were born from *The Piñata Theory*™ and can be found on Charlene's website.

Charlene has served the community for twenty-four years through her singing, music, volunteerism, and career in law enforcement. Charlene was honored with several awards for outstanding dedication to the community, including saving a life. She is a recognized leader who spearheaded several drug education projects, fundraisers and events.

Charlene loves to sing. She performed the US and Canadian national anthems for the Detroit Tigers and has sang at hundreds of events in Southwestern Ontario, Canada.

Charlene hosted her first live talk show — The Charlene & Co. Victory Celebration in 2017, featuring women who shared powerful stories about perseverance and achieving victory over adversity.

Charlene's work has been featured on Canadian television and radio, including CBC, CTV, Global TV, National Post, Windsor Star, CKSY, CFCO, CKLW, CFPL, New WI, Q107, City TV, Ontario Provincial Police Review and more.

Charlene Renaud – Professional Speaker, Author, Life Coach

www.charlenerenaud.com
info@charlenerenaud.com
Tel: 519-436-3911 (Canada)

Made in the USA
Middletown, DE
24 July 2018